Justice in the Mountains

Justice in the Mountains

Stories and Tales
by a
Vermont Country Lawyer

Deane C. Davis

Illustrated by Sue Storey

The New England Press
Shelburne, Vermont

The New England Press, Inc.
P.O. Box 525
Shelburne, Vermont 05482

Library of Congress Catalog Card Number: 80-82866
ISBN (cloth) 0-933050-05-4
ISBN (paper) 0-933050-06-2

The author and the publisher are grateful to the following publications for their permission to use material in this book:

Country Journal, "Nothing But the Truth," March, 1979; *Vermont Life Magazine,* "As Well Be Hung for a Sheep," Autumn, 1980; *Yankee Magazine,* "The Motter," November, 1980.

First printing, November 1980
Second printing, January 1981

Printed by Queen City Printers Inc., Burlington, Vermont
PRINTED IN THE UNITED STATES OF AMERICA

iv

Introduction

Vrest Orton

U.S. Senator Stephen A. Douglas, born in Brandon, Vermont, in 1813, carved for himself a permanent niche in the pantheon of American politics with his historic debates that propelled Abraham Lincoln into the presidency and with a remark Douglas uttered in 1851 when he returned to his native state and spoke in Brandon. At this public reception Senator Douglas exclaimed: "I love the old Green Mountains and valleys of Vermont....My friends, Vermont is the most glorious spot on the face of this globe for a man to be born in, provided he emigrates when he is very young."

This witticism has been debated by historians for over a century, but facts demonstrate that Senator Douglas spoke with more truth than jest. As a proof of this assertion, the prestigious *Dictionary of American Biography*, which includes only Americans who have made significant and notable contributions to life in the United States, lists 329 Vermonters. And most of these did indeed leave Vermont to become famous. Where they would have ended up had they stayed in the state of their birth is idle speculation.

But there is no idle speculation about the national fame of

one native Vermonter who achieved it without leaving the Green Mountain State and who earned it in four different professions.

I am talking about Deane Chandler Davis, the author of this book.

I believe that it is important to set down here a brief summary of his four occupations, in each of which he achieved undeniable success. This statement has been questioned by some of my friends who say, "Everyone knows all about Deane Davis, you don't need to tell them." It is very true that every one of his contemporaries has followed his four careers, but we now have on hand two new generations who may be reading this book and who should know something of the author's background.

Admitted to the Vermont bar when he was twenty-two years old (in 1922), Governor Davis practiced law in Vermont courts for eighteen years, taking time to serve as Barre City attorney and as state's attorney for Washington County, as well as on various boards and in public affairs. Except for his terms of office as prosecuting attorney for town and county, Attorney Davis chalked up a record as one of Vermont's outstanding trial lawyers.

His record won him the appointment as judge of the Vermont Superior Court when he was only thirty-one years old. I believe that he was one of the two youngest Vermonters ever to sit on that bench. Here he served for five years.

In 1940, Judge Davis began a long, distinguished, new career with the National Life Insurance Company of Montpelier. This company was founded by the father of Admiral George Dewey and is one of the largest life insurance companies in the United States, as well as, in volume of business, the largest financial institution in Vermont. Here Deane Davis served as general counsel, then president and chief executive officer, and finally chairman of the board and chief executive officer until 1968.

While serving as chief executive officer of National Life, he established a national reputation in the life insurance industry, having served as head of two major national organizations—The Life Insurance Association of America and The Institute of Life Insurance. During that time, he also served terms on the Education Committee of the American College and the Board of Trustees of the Life Underwriters Training Council. A professional educational contribution was his book *Life Insurance and Business Purchase Agreements*, for many years a leading work on that subject. In 1961 he was designated Man of the Year by the magazine *Insurance Field* "in recognition for having made the greatest contribution to the Life Insurance Business in 1961."

In these busy years Governor Davis also took a prominent part in Republican state affairs. He was a delegate to national conventions, as well as chairman of the Vermont state Republican conventions during presidential election years. Hardly a year came that many of us in the Republican party did not urge him to run for governor—but always without success because he felt that he must complete his responsibility to National Life in Montpelier. When his friends were finally successful (or he gave in to the many implorings, I don't know which), in 1968 he was elected to the state's highest office and served until 1973.

In this fourth calling, I think that we may say without fear of contradiction from any political side, Deane Davis was one of the best governors we have had in the memory of anyone alive.

His accomplishments during two terms were marked by originality and success. The several years since 1973, when he left office, have amply demonstrated the value of his innovative policies. The sales tax had been discussed for some years with other governors as a necessary support for a state's sound fiscal position. Deane Davis was, however, the first governor of Vermont to exhibit the courage to sponsor and get through the General Assembly this urgently needed tax statute—a virtual necessity to deal with the deficit left by a previous administration. It was based on the fair policy of spreading sales taxation over a wide area in order to include millions of tourists whose visits to Vermont constitute our second largest economic sector.

Next, Governor Davis initiated and signed Public Law 250. This act today is generally acknowledged to be the first and the best in the nation, as well as the fairest and most effective way to protect a state's natural resources and, at the same time, avoid stifling reasonable and healthy economic growth.

His third achievement was in the area of the administration of state goverment. Governor Davis, after a careful study in depth of the state's needs in the administration of the laws and the promotion of the public interest, persuaded the legislature to put into effect an efficient and workable cabinet form of state government at the executive level. All three of Governor Davis's policies are in practice today.

So we sum up: four different professions, all without leaving the state where he was born.

And now a fifth.

With this book Deane Davis has become an author. How does a busy man (or anyone else) become an author?

By writing and reading.

Governor Davis has told me about his reading. When he came home from Boston University Law School to start practicing in Barre, his father, who was also a lawyer and proud possessor of a liberal education, was disappointed that his son had not grounded himself long enough in liberal arts even though he had taken a law degree. The father gave some advice. "Establish a habit," he told his son, "of reading a minimum of one hour each day. It doesn't matter what you read because first you have to establish the habit. Then read with concentration. Concentrate on ideas, not words. Your interests will widen as your perceptions strengthen."

This good counsel the son followed all his life. In the broad scope of his reading he discovered great authors. One of his favorites was Justice Oliver Wendell Holmes of the U.S. Supreme Court. Holmes's book on the common law, for example, is a classic in not only the law but American literature because of the facility with which the Justice expressed himself.

I believe that Governor Davis has lived up to Justice Holmes's stipulation that "the life of the law has not been logic: it has been experience." Deane Davis's long experience in the courts of Vermont from both sides (the bar and the bench) helped to shape the wealth of his achievement in the insurance business and as governor.

I am also mindful that Justice Holmes declared: "The riders in the race do not stop short when they reach the goal. There is a little finishing canter before coming to a standstill. . . . Life is to function. . . . That is all there is to living." I feel sure that Governor Davis, as an ardent owner and promoter of Vermont's famous Morgan horses and formerly president of the Morgan Horse Association, appreciates Holmes's figure of speech.

If Deane Davis had stopped short at the end of any one of his careers, it is indeed a reasonable conclusion that we would not be experiencing the joy of reading this book.

One becomes an author also by writing. Busy men in the law, on the bench, and in private business don't pass a day without writing something. Being the author of this book of experiences of a trial lawyer and judge, however, is another matter entirely. In this undertaking one needs talent to project and make people come alive and also to convey to the reader ideas and often comic and sometimes tragic quirks and idiosyncrasies of human nature. In this book Attorney and Judge Davis has demonstrated this talent. I use these two titles advisedly. The reminiscences that make this book so delightful deal only with his years in court, both as a lawyer and on the bench.

After reading these typical Vermont tales, I feel sure that all Vermonters will express the hope that in the years to come Governor Davis will also find time to write about his life in the other two professions to which he has made distinguished contributions.

I end this introduction without doing what most writers of introductions attempt to do: that is, to explain to the reader what the author is doing.

I consider that task is, as it should be, the prerogative of the author.

Preface

Justice Oliver Wendell Holmes once wrote that "the life of the law has not been logic—it has been experience."

Trial by jury, for those involved, is a moment of intensive living. For spectators, it is more like a dramatic production, with one important distinction—there is no script. It simply evolves as a picture of human conflicts is painted, replete with action, pathos, humor, and sometimes sadness, and with an ending that no one can know for sure until it has ended. It is often full of surprises.

Most of the incidents portrayed in this book were matters in which I was personally involved as counsel or incidents that happened in my presence. The remainder are stories frequently told around the courthouses under circumstances that offered a presumption of their validity. But as to this latter group, I cannot, of course, vouch for their accuracy.

All of these stories are offered as an illustration of country law practice in earlier days when our system had not yet reached the level of its modern sophistication. For that reason I believe they are a pertinent part of the ongoing history of the evolution of life in Vermont.

Many of the names of characters have been changed to avoid possible embarrassment.

To my wife Marjorie
for her patience, understanding, and affection.

Contents

Justice in the Mountains

Nothing But the Truth

In those long lost and much lamented horse-and-buggy days, a substantial part of the time of a Vermont lawyer was taken up with the giving of advice concerning the legal rights of unfortunate parties to horse trades. In every swap there was always at least one unfortunate party. Many of these cases were tried in court, but a far greater number never reached the actual litigation stage.

Winning that kind of a case before a Vermont jury was not an easy matter for a plaintiff. This was not because Vermont juries were disinclined to see justice done. It was simply that in those nostalgic days a very special kind of philosophy had grown up as to just what was justice in a horse trade. The law of Vermont, as to deceit and misrepresentation, in exchange of horses was not different from the law of misrepresentation in any other kind of transaction, but the juries applied it differently, and in doing so they were no less sincere in the execution of their duties. They merely applied the law in the light of a well understood standard of conduct that happened to differ from what was generally considered fair play in other types of transactions.

In those days almost everybody owned and used a horse, either for work or driving. Because it is a peculiarity of horses that, seemingly, there never was one that did not have at least one defect of structure or habit, and because also a great proportion of these defects were of the latent kind, horse trading in those days was a vocation for some, an avocation for others, and at least occasionally a downright necessity for still others. In any event it was extremely common.

So in Vermont every community had at least one man who earned his living "swapping horses." In the vernacular he was called a "horse jockey." As here used the phrase did not mean, as the word would imply elsewhere, one who drove or rode a horse in races. It meant simply one who made his principal business that of trading horses. How the phrase came to be so employed in Vermont has never been clear to me. I suspect that one reason was that a good horse jockey almost invariably came to possess exceptional ability in handling vicious horses and in curing vices, lameness, and other physical defects or diseases. Where the condition was necessarily chronic these masters of an abandoned art were most skillful in covering up defects at least long enough to consummate a sale or exchange. Even to those who made a business of it, horse trading was very much a game. These horse jockeys loved the game so much that they did a great deal of trading with each other.

One of the peculiarities of the profession was that a horse that had such a serious defect that he was wholly unusable was worth much more than a good one, if the defect was of such a kind that it could be covered up temporarily. Such horses were called "traders." Every jockey had at least one of these, which he valued highly. Its value lay in the fact that it could be sold or swapped easily and at a good price, and shortly the purchaser would come back to trade again, being then willing to get rid of the animal on almost any terms. On the second trade the original purchaser would rarely admit that he had discovered the defect. His declared reason for wanting to trade again would be that he found the horse "too fast" or "too slow" for his needs. Nor, on such occasions, would the jockey mention his knowledge of the horse's short-comings, but invariably he would put an extremely low value on the horse for some other reason. For example, he would probably say that he was "filled up" with horses, or he would explain how horses of this type didn't seem to be in demand. Of course, neither party deceived the other in the least. These "traders" were well known to all horse jockeys for miles around. There were certain ethics in the profession, among which was the principle that one horse jockey should not take in trade a "trader" that was known to be the "trader" of a brother horse jockey. The rather uniform observance of this rule was one reason why the innocent party who had bought the "trader" almost always came back to the jockey from whom he had recieved it.

In the sale of any article other than a horse, it is considered to be unfair dealing to fail to disclose latent defects and even more so to take active means to cover up a defect. Not so in Vermont in a horse trade. Doing so stemmed from the Vermonter's philosophy of individualism. A man was supposed to look out for himself. He knew, or ought to know, that the horse jockey would put one over on him if he could, and, being forewarned, he was expected to be forearmed. If he was not sufficiently forearmed to protect himself, it was considered to be better to let him suffer the burden of deception, that he might grow in "wisdom and stature" and thus be better forearmed come another day. So deceiving the other party by any means short of actual false statements was considered perfectly proper. Either party to the trade was held strictly accountable for a false statement, but it had to be shown to be clearly false. Thus double talk came to be developed into one of the higher and finer arts. Perhaps contemporary members of Congress drew their first lessons from these Vermont horse jockeys. The words had to be literally false; actual and intentional deceit was not enough.

Henry White, a Scotch blacksmith, had traded his sorrel mare with Will Batchelder. Will was a Vermont horse jockey of the old school. Henry had received in exchange a fine looking, fat bay mare. The trade had taken place in the yard in front of McLeod's Blacksmith Shop where Henry worked. As Henry hitched the bay mare up to his own buggy after his day's work was finished, he felt quite pleased with himself. He had been trying to get rid of the sorrel for some time, and now he had a fine looking mare, and the exchange had only cost him ten dollars "to boot." He took great satisfaction in thinking that now he wouldn't have to worry about those frequent cases of colic to which the sorrel was subject, or those frequent occasions when the sorrel would be so sore in her front feet that he would have to lay her up to rest just when he needed to use her most. As Henry drove through the village street on his way home, he was "all smiles" and a trifle self-satisfied as his friends eyed his new driving horse. His satisfaction was short-lived, however.

About a mile out of the village he started up Jockey Hollow Hill. Before the horse had negotiated more than a few hundred feet of the steep hill she was obviously in distress. Her sides were heaving and she was blowing through her nostrils. In a few minutes the mare staggered and fell on her side. Various ministrations were performed for the relief of the mare by Henry and others who gathered at the scene. All efforts were unavailing, and finally a call was dispatched for the veterinarian.

6

"Where'd you get this one?" asked Dr. Bancroft, as he completed his examination.

"From Will Batchelder," replied Henry.

"Did he tell you anything about the mare having the heaves?"

"I asked him about the heaves, and he said she did not have the heaves."

"Well, she's got the heaves, and it's the worst case I ever saw. She ain't worth a cent, and you might as well put her out of the way. I can get her back on her feet for you, but she'll never be able to do a tap of work. It's been a long time since she has been able to do a tap."

By the time Henry had arrived at my office the next day, his indignation had reached the boiling point. The pecuniary loss was bad enough, but what really elevated his blood pressure was the sense of humiliation at being bested in a horse trade under such circumstances that the whole town must know about it.

"I want him sued, and I don't care what it costs."

"How about this sorrel of yours, Henry? Were there any 'outs' about her?"

"Well, she was a little mite sore for'ard, and she had the colic once in awhile if you fed her too quick after she worked."

"Did you tell Will about that?"

"Hell, no. He never asked me."

"Did he tell you anything about this bay mare having the heaves?"

"Sure, he did. He said she didn't have the heaves."

"How'd he happen to tell you that?"

"Well, I asked him."

"How'd you happen to ask him?"

"Well, I couldn't see how he was so willing to trade for ten dollars to boot. So I asked him quite a lot of questions. I

7

asked him if she was 'heavey,' and he said she wasn't."

"Did anybody hear Will tell you that?"

Henry thought a few minutes. "No, I guess not. Part of the trade was in the blacksmith shop, and there were several who heard that part, but we was out in the yard looking over the bay when I asked him about the heaves, and just the two of us were there then."

"Well, Henry, I'll bring your suit for you, but don't be too optimistic about winning. If Will denies that he told you the mare didn't have the heaves, it will be your word against his, and the jury has to be shown in a horse trade."

I brought the suit, and shortly the day of trial arrived. As we were impaneling the jury I grew less confident by the minute. It looked so easy for Will to deny that he had had any conversation about the mare's heaves, and I felt sure that the jury would not award a verdict for the plaintiff on the unsupported word of Henry. Because it was clear that the only hope was to get some sort of an admission out of Will, I decided to put him on the stand for cross-examination as the very first witness.

Will looked very confident and relaxed as he took his seat after receiving the oath administered by Judge Scott. I am sure that I looked as hopeless as I felt.

"Will, did you trade horses with the plaintiff recently?"

"Yes, sir."

"When was it?"

"July 21st last."

"Will you describe the horse you traded to the plaintiff?"

"She was a bay mare, about 15—2, weighed around eleven hundred."

"How long had you owned her?"

"Around ten days."

"Had you driven her much?"

"Oh, some."

"Taken any long trips with her?"

"No, sir."

"Driven her up any hills while you had her?"

"Yes, once."

"Was her wind sound?"

"No, it wasn't."

This was fine up to this point, but the real test was what he would say about the talk he had had with Henry.

"Did you have any talk with Henry about whether this mare had the heaves or not?"

I should explain here that the heaves is a disease of the respiratory tract in horses similar to asthma or emphysema in humans. It is usually incurable and progressive and disabling.

I definitely expected Will to answer my question in the negative, and no one was more surprised than I was when he answered, "Yes, sir."

He was not in the least disturbed by the question, and now a new fear assailed me. Would I dare to ask the next question as to what the talk was? It was obvious that there was no escape for me. I just had to ask the question that everyone in the courtroom was waiting for. How I dreaded to ask it!

"Tell us, Will, just what the talk was."

"Well, we was out looking at the mare, and Henry was asking all sorts of questions. He asked me if the horse had ever gone lame, if she was a kicker, if she was a cribber, and a whole lot of questions like that. Then he says, 'Will, has this horse got the heaves?' And I said, 'Henry, if this horse has got the heaves, I got the heaves.'"

At this point Will turned slowly to the jury, looked them straight in the eye, and said, in an unmistakably asthmatic voice, "And, by God, gentlemen, I have got the heaves."

Where There's a Will There's a Way

The rigid requirements of the Vermont statute relative to the formalities to be observed in execution of a will sometimes result in injustice to those who were the objects of the testator's bounty. Sometimes the law can be stretched to avoid injustice. Juries do it frequently and on the whole quite intelligently. Judges are more reluctant to take liberties in this way, but even judges have been known to do a little stretching when the end to be served is justice in the broad but very real sense.

Susan Cranston was an elderly lady who lived in Plainfield. The widow of John Cranston, she was much beloved by the people of the community. She had been the second wife of Cranston and had been a good mother to John's daughter, Mary, the fruit of John's first marriage. Mary had finally grown to womanhood, married, and had a daughter of her own. When John died he had left his whole estate consisting of about $75,000 to his wife, in full confidence that she would leave whatever was left when she should die to his daughter. Mrs. Cranston lived on for quite a few years, using the income of John's estate supplemented by her own meager earnings, which, however, were sufficient for her modest needs. In the meantime Mary's husband had died, and she left their home in Colorado and returned to Plainfield with her daughter to live with Mrs. Cranston. Mary had no property of her own but was able to earn enough to support herself and her daughter, Jane, and, of course, it was taken for granted that when Mrs. Cranston died the property would pass to Mary and Jane.

Then Mrs. Cranston was taken sick. She grew worse and finally developed pneumonia. One night the doctor told Mary that Mrs. Cranston had taken a very bad turn, and he feared that she would not live through the night. Mrs. Cranston, during her intermittent periods of consciousness, apparently realized how bad her condition was, for she asked that Mary send for Mr. Nelson. Nelson was a local merchant who held the office of justice of the peace. In every small Vermont town there is always an individual who acts as the unofficial representative of law and order, to whom people turn for advice on matters legal and quasi-legal, usually a pillar of respectability and possessed of more than average good sense. Such a man was Nelson. It was nearly midnight before Nelson could be reached, but he responded promptly as soon as he received the message.

"Frank," she said, "I guess I'm pretty sick. I've been wondering about the property. Of course, you know it was all John's property although I helped him save some of it, and since he died I haven't spent but a little of it except the interest, of course. Now what I want to know is, if I die, will it all go to Mary?"

"Haven't you made a will?" asked Nelson.

"Oh, no, I have never made a will. I supposed of course the property would go to John's daughter. It was mostly all his, you know."

"Yes, but when John died all of his property became yours, and you have the legal right to do whatever you want to with it. Now, of course, neither Mary nor Jane is your heir, and so, unless you have a will, the property will go to your heirs. Who are your heirs, anyway?"

"I really don't know who my heirs are," said Mrs. Cranston. "I have some second and third cousins, but they are scattered all over the country. I know where two or three of them are, but I haven't seen any of them for years and we don't even write."

"Then you'd better make a will. That's the only way you can pass the property on to Mary and Jane."

"Well, Frank, I want you to do whatever is necessary. You know what I want done, and I wish you would attend to it right away because I really think I'm pretty sick."

"It's pretty late to get a lawyer this time of night. You know them lawyers. They're worse than doctors. They don't like to work late at night, and they don't like to get out of bed."

Nelson went downstairs to the telephone and tried unsuccessfully to arouse a Montpelier lawyer. After trying three or four telephone numbers and getting no response, he went back upstairs. He was worrying about the situation. He knew the size of the property that Mrs. Cranston owned, and he realized what a tragedy it would be if the property were not to go where John had intended it. So he decided to take a chance and make the will himself. He didn't know just how to go at the task of drawing a will, having never been called on to do that sort of a job before. He did know that a will required three witnesses, and that is about all he did know about the requirements. This is what he wrote on the back of a piece of writing paper:

I hereby deed all of my property, real and personal,

to Frank Nelson, to be divided up and given to my stepdaughter, Mary George, and her daughter, Jane.

Nelson then had Mrs. Cranston sign this paper in the presence of the doctor, the nurse, and himself, and all three of them signed their names to the paper as witnesses. Before the night was over, Mrs. Cranston died.

A few weeks after Mrs. Cranston's death, Mr. Nelson and Mary drove to Montpelier with the paper that Mrs. Cranston had signed. They called to see the probate judge and handed him the document and explained the circumstances under which it had been signed. The judge examined it with sober countenance. After studying it for some time he turned to take down a couple of law books and spent several minutes turning the pages. He then turned to Nelson and Mary and said, "I'm sorry, but this instrument isn't a will. Maybe you can qualify it as a deed, but it certainly isn't a will."

"You mean it can't be probated?" said Nelson.

"That's just what I mean," said the judge. "You'd better take it to some lawyer, and maybe he can do something with it as a deed, but it certainly isn't a will, and I'm not going to have it filed here as a will."

Some weeks later Nelson and Mary called at my office with the document and explained the circumstances to me and what had happened at the time the paper was drawn. He also told me what the probate judge had said. They neglected to tell me that they had already consulted three other lawyers, who had advised them that the instrument was valueless. I confessed that I was somewhat baffled by the problem and so decided to do a little studying before I committed myself. Accordingly, I promised to look into the matter right away and see what, if anything, could be done.

My first impression was that the instrument might

perhaps be good enough to amount to a deed. The word *deed* was clearly written in the instrument. But, after examining the statutes and a number of decisions of the court construing the statutes, I was greatly disappointed to find that the law was pretty clear that, in such circumstances, the instrument would not be valid as a deed. Our statute requires that a deed to real estate shall be signed, sealed, witnessed by two witnesses, and acknowledged before a notary public or justice of the peace or other officer authorized to administer oaths. This instrument had an adequate number of witnesses and it was signed, but there was one fatal defect in that there was no acknowledgment whatsoever.

My next guess was that perhaps, though not valid as a legal deed, it might be held good in equity. Again, I was doomed to disappointment. Our rule in Vermont is clear that an instrument that is defective as a deed because it is not executed with the necessary formalities may in certain cases be held good in equity and a good deed compelled to be given. Where there is no valuable consideration and the instrument is in effect intended as a gift, equity will not intervene to make a good instrument of a bad instrument. The rule is otherwise where there is a valid consideration.

After reaching this conclusion I held the matter aside for a few days because I dreaded the task of telling Mary that her instrument was valueless, but I could not get the matter out of my mind. It seemed that the law must have some relief for a situation like this, where every dictate of common justice dictated that the property should go to Mary and her daughter. So I started searching for a precedent anywhere that might give us any support whatsoever for the validity of the instrument as a will. True, the probate judge had already ruled that it wasn't a will, but I knew that the probate judge was a man who would want to do real justice. After studying at odd moments for nearly a week, I finally located an opinion by the Supreme Court of the State of Pennsylvania, where a paper had been drawn that in substance was remarkably like the one in question. Even the word *deed* had been used in this case. The court in that case held that the instrument was ambiguous, and, being ambiguous, it was proper for the court to take parole evidence to determine what the true intention of the party signing it was. And where, as there, the court found from facts and circumstances surrounding the execution of the instrument that a will was intended instead of a deed, the instrument could be allowed as a will. True, we had a number of decisions in Vermont that were slightly inconsistent, although not squarely inconsistent, with that holding. It was all I could find, so I decided to do what I could with it.

I prepared a written petition to the Probate Court asserting that this instrument was a will and that it had been duly and properly executed, and praying that the court would set a date for notice of hearing thereon, and I had the petition signed by Mr. Nelson and by Mary. I took the petition to Montpelier and presented it to the probate judge. I also handed him the document that Mrs. Cranston signed.

"This instrument has been presented here before on four different occasions, and I have refused to file it every time. I am still refusing to file it. This isn't a will. It may be a deed, but it isn't a will. It hasn't got a word in it that even mentions or suggests that it is a will. There isn't a word in it to suggest that the intention of the maker is that the property shall pass at death, as distinguished from immediately."

"Well, of course, you may be right about that. Maybe it isn't a will, but this petition which I have handed you, signed by Mary, one of the beneficiaries, and by Nelson, also one of the beneficiaries, probably a trustee, asserts and alleges that it is a will. Under the circumstances it's your duty, whether you believe it's a will or not, to publish a notice on this petition and listen to the evidence before you decide the question," I said.

"What's the use of going through a foolish performance like that? It isn't a will, and you know it isn't a will."

"No, I don't know that it isn't a will. In fact, I'm claiming and shall prove that it is a will. Whether you believe it or not, you can't escape holding a hearing on the question of whether it is a due and valid will or not."

"Well, you can't make a damned fool out of this court," he said.

"Well, I can try. If you persist in refusing to issue a notice and to hold a hearing on this petition, I won't have to try very hard."

"Well, people can make a jackass out of me when I don't know any better, but they can't make a jackass out of me when I do know better, and this is one of the times when I do know better."

"Then you mean to say that you decide your cases before you have heard the evidence?"

"I've heard all the evidence I need. This is all the evidence there is."

"All right," I said. "You do whatever you want to do, but I'm leaving this petition right here, and you'd better study law a little while and see if you don't come to the conclusion that you can't avoid holding a hearing on this petition which I have filed." Saying that, I left the office.

In about three days I received a letter from the judge, saying very curtly that he had decided to issue an order of notice on the will and giving me the date on which the hearing was to be held, as provided by the notice. In his own handwriting at the bottom of the letter he had written, "This is still a lot of damn foolishness.''

Under Vermont practice where notice of a hearing is given by publication in a newspaper, as provided in the statute, all persons wherever situated are deemed to have had actual notice of the proceedings, and if they do not appear, even if they did not know about the hearing, they are bound by the judgment. So I knew that if I could only persuade the judge that this was a will, then, since no one would appear and contest the ruling, I was sure that that would establish the will as valid, whether the conclusion was correct as a matter of law or not. I recognized, however, by what had transpired that it was going to be no easy job to convince the judge that it was a will.

On the day of the hearing I had the doctor and the nurse and Mr. Nelson in court. I will also confess that I had spent considerable time with them, discussing the nature of their testimony. They were properly ''horse shedded,'' as we call it here in Vermont. One by one these witnesses were placed on the stand and asked to tell all the facts and circumstances surrounding the execution of the will and particularly to tell about the talk that occurred, in which Mrs. Cranston spoke about her intention and desire that the property on her death should go to Mary and Jane, and the fact that she had used the word *will* again and again in her discussion. The judge kept breaking into the testimony with statements to the effect that this was all inadmissible but he supposed that he would have to listen to it. At the conclusion of the testimony I excused all the witnesses and all the parties so that I might have a chance to argue the case with the probate judge without being under the embarrassment of the presence of other people. There was, of course, no appearance on the other side, so it was just a matter of the judge and me together.

''Now you are a man who believes in justice, aren't

you?'' I asked. He admitted that he was. "Now, you'll admit that the broad justice of this case is that this property ought to go to Mary and Jane in some way. That's what ought to be done, isn't it?''

"Yes,'' he said, "but if people are so careless and ignorant that they don't follow the law, what can I do?''

"You admit, then, that the real justice of this case is that the property ought to go to Mary and Jane. Now, it can't go to Mary and Jane unless this court holds that this is a will. Now, when you are satisfied that the broad justice of a case demands a certain result, isn't it fair for the probate judge to lean over backwards a little way to see to it that justice is done?''

"Well, that depends on how far he has to lean.''

"Well, in a case like this, if you could find a court of last resort in one of the large states of the country that had held that an instrument practically the same as this was a will under the circumstances as here, you would feel that maybe there was a little doubt in your mind as to whether you are right that this is not a will, wouldn't you?''

"Sure,'' he said, "if I could find any good excuse for holding this a will, then I would do it.''

"Well, here's your excuse, Judge. This is a court of last resort of the State of Pennsylvania, one of the best of the appellate courts in the country.''

I had brought the original volume in which the case was reported and handed it to him to read. He read it slowly and then he read it again. Then he got up and walked around the courtroom once or twice and came back, sat down, and read it again.

"Well,'' he said, "I'll have to think about this.''

I didn't argue any further because I could see by the expression on his face that I was making headway. I decided it was best not to press the advantage, and so I left and went back to my office. During the afternoon of the next day I received a letter from the probate judge with the words in it: "It's a will."

Of course the property was decreed to Mr. Nelson as trustee for the benefit of Mary and Jane, and the trustee immediately turned the property over to Mary and Jane and filed a report.

And justice was done.

The Price of Tears

Ronnie Harvey, as he was called, was an unusually skillful trial lawyer who lived in Montpelier and practiced law in the horse-and-buggy days. His practice covered both Washington and Orange counties, and he had an enviable reputation as a lawyer. He hated office work and gradually became known as the lawyer who practiced law from his buggy.

On Monday mornings he would hitch up his handsome pair of chestnut Morgan horses and travel the countryside of Washington and Orange counties, usually returning home on Thursday afternoons. He spent the week visiting clients, interviewing witnesses, drawing deeds, contracts, and wills, and giving advice along the way. He usually stayed for meals and overnight with his clients as there were no hotels in the area he covered. He was probably Vermont's best-known itinerant lawyer.

When he wasn't traveling the roads he was in court trying jury cases. He was a much-sought-after lawyer and most successful.

One of his peculiarities was a minor physical affliction of the eyelids that made it possible for him to "turn on the

tears'' at his slightest wish. Most people did not realize that this was an affliction but regarded it as a part of his oratorical power. Whenever the emotional content of his case made it desirable to whip up sympathy for his client he could cry with deep and moving effect upon the jury.

In Orange county he was trying a contested will case for his client, Abe Jacobs, a Corinth farmer. Abe was the descendant of a little-known Jewish man, who came to Vermont as an itinerant pack peddler, stayed overnight with one of his Corinth farmer customers, and never left until he had married the farmer's daughter.

The case was a particularly emotional one. Ronnie's argument to the jury was said to be one of the greatest forensic examples ever to occur in Orange county court. Ronnie's client won.

After court adjourned, Abe stood on the courthouse steps receiving the congratulations of the spectators as they filed out on their way home.

One of the spectators, speaking to Abe, remarked, ''And wasn't that the most wonderful speech there when Mr. Harvey cried and the tears streamed down his face?''

''Yes,'' said Abe, ''it was wonderful. But you know every one of those tears is going to cost me five dollars each.''

As Well Be Hung for a Sheep

David Brown and his wife lived on a farm in the Town of Topsham. David was not a farmer in the real sense, for he earned his living as a schoolteacher. His wife was a talented artist, and, from their joint earnings, David and his wife had purchased the "old home place" where David had been born, and they had rebuilt the farmhouse into a very comfortable home.

Their farming operations consisted entirely of raising sheep. It cannot be said that the farming operations were successful in the economic sense, because each year the accounts showed a substantial loss. The reason for the losses was simple. Mrs. Brown loved each lamb and could never bring herself to part with a single one. Every sheep was an individual, and she knew them all by name. In such an atmosphere it was not surprising that the flock contained as many "bucks" as "ewes"—a principle that does not work well in sheep raising. But David and Mary were not at all disturbed by the yearly losses. They felt well repaid by the mutual exchange of love and affection between themselves and the "lambies."

One night in late November, David and his wife returned home from an automobile ride just at dusk. As was his custom, David went to the pasture gate to let the sheep into the barn to protect them from the chilly night. Mary stood by, counting each one as it came through the gate, murmuring little messages of endearment and calling them by name. As the last one trotted by, Mary suddenly spoke, "David, there's only sixty-eight. There should be sixty-nine."

"Oh, you must have made a mistake," said David, as he closed the gate. "Maybe one slipped by that you didn't see. Let's go into the barn and count them again."

A second and third count, however, still showed one unaccounted for.

"It's Susie," said Mary. "She just isn't here. Where in the world can she be?"

"Let's go up in the pasture and have a look," said David. "Maybe she didn't come down to the gate. Don't worry, we'll find her."

So they went into the pasture, calling "Susie, Susie, come Susie," as they traveled over the rough pasture land, making a systematic search. Suddenly Mary stopped and called to David in a horror-stricken voice, "David, come here quick. See what I've found."

David hurried to his wife's side, and his worst apprehensions were verified as he saw what Mary had found. There on the frozen ground was a copious quantity of fresh blood and the entrails of an animal that had been recently slaughtered. Mary burst into tears, and David stared with unbelieving eyes.

"Oh, David, who could have done such a horrible thing?"

"We'll soon find out. I'm going to get the sheriff. You go back to the house and get supper. I'll be back as quick as I can."

David hurried to get his car and drove to the village with little regard for the speed limit or the rough and winding road. Carl Stone was the sheriff's deputy who represented the law in Topsham. What he lacked in scientific training for criminal investigation was more than compensated for by his Yankee shrewdness and his thorough and detailed knowledge of the habits, characters, and propensities of the Topsham citizenry. He had brought many a violator to justice by the "Stone System." So far as is known this system has never been approved by any recognized school of police method, but in spite of its unorthodox character it often worked, and it had saved Carl many tedious hours and much shoe leather.

Carl's system was simple. When a complaint was made he would listen patiently to the story of the crime. Then he would close his eyes and say to himself, "Now, let's see who would do a job like that." Out of the vast reservoir of his subconscious mind would slowly emerge the image of one after another of his townspeople. As each image of a resident was flashed on the screen of Carl's conscious mind, he would review in restrospect his or her past history, character, temperament, and circumstances. Usually this process of selection would eventually produce a candidate whose known habits and propensities would fit the story of the crime, and Carl would then go ahead and question the suspect and eventually get a confession. Often this would happen when there was not a shred of legal evidence to connect the suspect to the crime.

The deputy and David drove to the scene of the crime "to view the corpus delicti," as Carl put it. Carl looked the ground over and listened to David's incoherent account of the search for Susie and the discovery of the blood and some of the remains. Carl walked slowly around the vicinity searching the ground. Eventually his search was rewarded. A short distance from the scene of the crime Carl found a few tracks in a thin covering of snow that had not been melted by the sun. These few tracks pointed in a generally westerly direction. This was the direction one would take to the home of John Jackson, one of David's more distant neighbors. Probably not even Carl could tell whether it was the tracks or the knowledge of Jackson's habits and propensities that suggested to Carl the desirability of making a call on Jackson. At any rate, he told David to go back to the house and eat his supper. "I'm going to make a call," he said.

Jackson was a rather harmless ne'er-do-well who lived in one of the houses that had been abandoned by the company when Pike Hill Copper Mines closed down permanently. He rarely worked but always got along somehow. It was generally believed that the simple needs of his small family were mainly supplied by picking up items with little regard to the "fiction" of legal ownership.

"Oh, hello, Carl," said Jackson, as he opened the door in response to the deputy's knock. "Come in. Glad to see you." This last was probably an overstatement.

Carl went in, greeted Mrs. Jackson, took the offered chair in the kitchen, and chatted for a while as he looked the situation over. Noticing a boiling pot on the stove, he walked over and lifted the lid. "Mutton, huh?" There was no answer from either Jackson or his wife, but Carl had no difficulty diagnosing that characteristic expression of sullen apprehension that was registered so plainly on both their faces.

"Well, John, I'm sorry, but you'll have to get your hat and coat. The law's the law and I have no choice."

Carl took Jackson in his car and, after leaving word for David to come to the village, drove to Waits River and assembled the various cogs that constituted the machinery of rural justice in action. The town grand juror, Vermont's unique kind of rural prosecuting officer, was notified, and shortly all assembled in the one and only country store of the village, which was operated by Henry Lawson, the justice of the peace. There are approximately 1,700 of these justices in the state of Vermont, although only a fraction of that number ever actually perform any duties as such, and only a much smaller fraction ever have the temerity to "hold court." But Lawson was a real trial justice, made so by the necessities of his environment.

It was a colorful and pungent courtroom. Shelves of canned goods lined the walls; molasses barrels, sugar barrels, stacks of flour, and racks filled with clothing and shoes covered the floor. The pungent odors from this miscellany mingled with those from the kerosene pump and combined to perfect that comfortable, suggestive, tantalizing, and truly characteristic smell that, once smelled, can never be forgotten. The long counter made a convenient workbench, and, after a more or less general discussion of the facts in the case, Justice Lawson pulled down from a shelf behind the counter the *Vermont Public Laws*, which constituted the court's complete library. Of course, there used to be several smaller books containing the amendments and additions made at the biennial sessions of the legislature since the publication of the *Public Laws*, but these had been found inconvenient to use and so had been gradually mislaid and forgotten. As Lawson once said, "There's all the law we need in that big book, so why bother with any more? Besides, those little books mostly contradict what's in the big book and get you all mixed up."

Lawson opened the "big book" and spread it out on the counter, put on his spectacles, and began to run through the index. Above the counter two large kerosene lamps shed an uncertain light. Around the counter, in various stages of posture, some seated on barrels, stood and sat the official and unofficial participants in the drama. In addition to the justice, Fred Town (the grand juror), Carl, and Jackson (the respondent), there were four or five villagers who had straggled in, attracted by the store lights and anxious to see what was going on. Even these uninvited guests seemed to be conscious of a certain responsibility to see that the dignity of the law was upheld.

Lawson first turned to "Homicide" but quickly discovered that subject inapplicable because there was no mention of sheep.

"Try 'Sheep,'" offered Town, who as prosecutor had a special duty to perform.

Lawson finally found "Sheep" in the index and was referred to Section ———. "Here it is. Now let's see." As some of the others looked over his shoulder, he read:

> A person who suffers loss by the worrying, maiming or killing of his sheep by dogs, within twenty-four hours after he learns of such damage, shall give notice thereof to one or more of the selectmen who shall appraise the amount (of damage). Such appraisal shall be for the full value of the animals killed, not less than one-half value of all animals maimed and not less than fifty cents per head for any injury to the remainder of the flock caused by worrying.

A sharp discussion ensued as to the applicability of that statute to the case at hand, which was finally settled by the justice who stated, "No, it don't fit. There wan't no dog."

During the more heated part of the argument, Jackson, who had been looking over the shoulder of the justice, appropriated the *Public Laws* and carefully studied various sections as he occasionally turned the pages, wholly oblivious to the debate that was going on around him.

"Here's what you want," said Jackson, "Section 3. It's petit larceny, that's what it is. Stealing, taking or carrying away personal property of a value of less than twenty-five dollars."

The justice again put on his spectacles and read aloud the section referred to.

"But that don't say anything about the killing," said David. "I'm not interested in the value. It's the killing of Susie that I want to see punished. In one way it's just as bad as killing a person. Mary and I thought more of Susie than we do of a good many people."

"Well, we got something that covers anyway," said Justice Lawson. "A sheep is personal property, and I guess the goin' prices of any sheep would be less than twenty-five dollars. Anyway, we'll put a mark here so we can find it again."

Then began a futile and prolonged search for some section that related specifically to the killing of a sheep.

"Tain't no use," said Lawson. "The only law to fit the case is petit larceny."

One of the spectators said later that he thought he detected a clear expression of satisfaction on Jackson's face, which at the time he laid to the fact that it was Jackson who had first discovered the section on petit larceny.

Fred Town, the grand juror, with the combined help of Justice Lawson and Carl, with an occasional suggestion from the spectators, finally produced what passed for a legal criminal complaint. It charged that Jackson on the day in question did "steal, take and carry away one sheep of the value of Five Dollars, named Susie, contrary to the statute and against the peace of the state." When this venerable document had been pleaded and signed by the grand juror and the warrant signed by the justice of the peace, Justice Lawson rapped for order in the courtroom and ordered the respondent to stand and listen to the reading of the complaint, which Jackson solemnly and obligingly did. The complaint was read slowly and deliberately, and at the conclusion of the reading Justice Lawson said, "To this complaint do you plead guilty or not guilty?"

It was no surprise to anyone in the room that Jackson's response was, "Guilty."

Then followed much discussion as to what the fine or other punishment should be. The judge finally announced that the fine would be five dollars and that court costs would be five dollars. Jackson began to dig into his various pockets. Coming up with many old and rusty coins, buttons, and so forth, he finally found enough money to pay the five dollar fine, but it was apparent that he could not pay the costs. Thereupon, Justice Lawson announced that the court would trust the respondent for the five dollar costs, which he must pay at the rate of one dollar per week. Court was adjourned without ceremony, and the respondent was left to find his way home on foot as best he could.

David delayed a little while to talk the situation over with his friends present in the store but finally drove home to have his supper. As he drove into the yard and alighted from his car, he was surprised to hear a very distinct bleating that seemed to come from the pasture. Hurrying to the pasture gate to satisfy his curiosity, he could hardly believe his eyes when he saw there by the gate, running up and down trying to get out, none other than Susie. He ran to the house to announce the good news to Mary. She was overjoyed, but David was perplexed. He had just witnessed a plea of guilty to the stealing of Susie by Jackson, and yet here she was alive and well.

He pondered the situation for some time and then announced with determination that he was going back to the village. There was something wrong about the case. He hurried to the home of the justice of the peace and told his story. The justice telephoned Carl and the grand juror, and they hurried to Lawson's house. After considering the situation and discussing it at length, they decided that Carl should go and return Jackson to Lawson's house for further questioning. Carl drove to Jackson's home and reached it just as Jackson was completing the last lap of the two and a half miles of steady walking uphill to get there. He took Jackson, who made no protest, into the car and returned to the home of Justice Lawson. By this time it was eleven o'clock at night. The justice explained to Jackson that Susie had been found.

"Now we want to know, Jackson, what's the real story on this? What actually happened anyhow?"

Jackson remained silent and refused to answer. One by one the sheriff, the justice, and David took a hand in questioning Jackson. All he would say was, "I pled guilty, didn't I?"

The evening wore on. The tempers of the participants grew more touchy by the minute but still Jackson refused to talk. Finally the justice had an inspiration. "Jackson, I told you the court would trust you for the amount of those costs, but on account of your attitude and because you won't talk, I'm going to countermand that order right now. You're in the custody of the court, and unless you are willing to talk and tell us the story, I'm going to order you committed to jail, and Carl will take you over to Chelsea and lock you up."

This was an alternative that Jackson had not reckoned with. His countenance showed that the prospect was not at all pleasant for him to contemplate. Finally he said, "Well, I guess I might as well tell you the story. You see, the fact is that I was over in the pasture with my rifle today, and I run across a big five-point buck. Of course, it's out of season, but I didn't have any meat, so I took a shot and got him the first crack. I dressed him off and carried him home, and it was a piece of that meat that you saw boiling on the stove."

"But why in the world did you plead guilty?" said Lawson.

"Well, you see when we was alooking over the book there in the store I see in the book that the minimum fine for shooting a deer out of season was one hundred dollars, and the minimum fine for petit larceny was five dollars. What would you do in a situation like that?"

A Blow for Freedom

In this day of extensive regulation of individuals by the state, it is refreshing to be reminded that there still exist constitutional restraints upon the power of the state in its dealings with individuals. One of these restraints is the constitutional doctrine that no man shall be required to give evidence against himself. This principle was formulated in a day when men feared loss of liberty by excessive exercise of governmental power to a far greater extent than is the case today. Indeed, it is difficult to believe that such a doctrine should be written into the basic law of the land if a new constitution were being written today, so callous are the people of the manifold encroachments of government upon the areas of freedom of individual action. The rule that "no man shall be required to give evidence against himself" is applicable even if the party in whose favor it is exercised is known to be guilty. In fact, the rule practically assumes the guilt.

Mary Shady was a Lebanese lady who was said to have operated a flourishing "kitchen bar" during the late lamented days of Prohibition. Some people believed that she not only possessed the special art or skill of selecting the proper brands of liquor to satisfy the taste of discriminating Barre customers but also—what was perhaps of equal importance, if she was to stay in business—the technique for circumventing detection and conviction. This technique had its many fine points, but mainly it was built on two rules of practice. The first was to permit access only to those customers who were known by character, temperament, and experience to be trusted not to "peach" even if it became necessary to commit perjury. The second was to keep the current "supply" on a shelf beside the kitchen sink, so that if the officers of the law, bearing a search warrant, made a sudden and unexpected appearance, the bottles containing the supply could be quickly broken in the kitchen sink, pass down the drainpipe, and thus leave only a smell, which, though readily identified by the officers, was peculiarly incapable of being marked as "Exhibit A" in court. Barre juries were extremely suspicious of the olfactory nerves of their raiding police officers and insisted on production of the corpus delicti before they would convict. Thus, customers were divided into two classes: those who could surely be relied upon "come Hell or high water," and those who had not yet won their spurs. The first group were entitled to sit in the parlor and be served by glass. The second group might purchase by the pint but never would be allowed in the house.

Forrest Hull and Ernest Tomasi were two young men not quite twenty-one years of age who belonged to the second group. On a certain dark night they each purchased a pint of whiskey just inside the back door and started to leave the premises, little knowing that two burly guardians of the law were lurking in the shadows across the way, well concealed from view but able to observe the comings and goings of thirsty customers. Hardly had Hull and Tomasi reached the public street when they found themselves in the custody of two officers who quickly relieved them of the two pints, transported the prisoners to the police station, and there questioned them at length as to what had occurred just previous to their rude apprehension.

The boys were wholly oblivious to the historical fact that the Founding Fathers had inserted the aforementioned provision in the Constitution in anticipation of just such circumstances as these, and so they readily admitted that they had purchased the liquor from Mrs. Shady and that each had paid $2.50 a pint therefor. They obligingly signed a written statement to this effect and in exchange were permitted to quit the jail, which they quickly did.

In due course Mrs. Shady was apprehended on a warrant and complaint charging that she did "sell intoxicating liquor, contrary to the form, force and effect of the statute in such case made and provided and against the peace and dignity of the state." She was arraigned before the Municipal Court, Judge H. W. Scott presiding, and, upon being acquainted with the nature of the accusation, pleaded "not guilty" in righteous indignation. She gave bail in the sum of $300 for her later appearance at trial and came to my office seeking counsel to conduct her defense.

I felt some reluctance to undertake Mrs. Shady's defense. This reluctance did not stem from any mistaken notions of ethics, for, after all, I knew and well understood the fact that a lawyer's duty in such circumstances is to give his or her client the best defense possible no matter how strong may be the suspicion that the client is guilty. No, the reluctance arose from the fact that the chances were about one hundred to one that Mrs. Shady would be convicted. Young lawyers hate to take a licking. As a matter of fact, so do old ones. It was a matter of general knowledge that Mrs. Shady had several times before been convicted of violations of the liquor laws.

That fact was known altogether too well to Judge Scott, who, to say the least, was not disposed to strain the quality of mercy in favor of those who trafficked in intoxicating liquors, much less to one who had been before him on several previous occasions.

Recognizing that the case was desperate, I called in my old friend Albert A. Sargent, whose knowledge of human nature, experience in the field of criminal law, and general all-around ability and capacity for masterful strategy in hopeless cases has been a source of inspiration to me ever since I started practice. Albert readily agreed to associate himself with me in the case in accordance with his regular custom, which was always to accept the most hopeless cases with enthusiasm. After several conferences the strategy was agreed on.

Clearly, the only hope to cheat the law of its victim was to exclude the testimony of the two boys whose thirst had been so rudely thwarted. This method of procedure was based necessarily upon the assumption that the state would have no other evidence except the testimony of the two boys. We were not entirely sure that this was the fact, but, after all, in criminal cases you have to take some chances. Accordingly, we called in the two boys and examined them at length as to the facts and circumstances surrounding the purchase of the liquor, their apprehension, and the statements that they had signed for the officers.

"Do you boys have any hard feelings against Mrs. Shady?" we asked.

They both said that they did not.

"Do you really want to testify against her?"

They both admitted that was the last thing in the world they wanted to do.

"But, what can we do?" said Hull. "We told the officers we bought the liquor and signed a paper, and the police have the two pints. They will make us tell it in court."

"Did you ever read the Constitution of the United States?" I asked.

"Do you mean the Declaration of Independence?" asked Hull. "I read that in school on Memorial Day, and I don't want to try it again."

"Well, the Constitution and the Declaration of Independence are not exactly the same, but we won't go into that just now. But the Constitution says that nobody has to give evidence against himself. Now, if you testify that you purchased the liquor and had possession of liquor, that is evidence tending to show that you yourself would be guilty of the crime of illegal possession of liquor. I think you boys need a good lawyer and need him bad."

"Yes," said Tomasi, "but the police let us go, and they knew we had the liquor. If that is so why did they let us go? They didn't have any right to let us go, did they?"

"Well, they are trying to fry bigger fish. Anyway, they can arrest you again anytime they want to. I think you had better see a good lawyer, and he will advise you that you don't need to testify against Mrs. Shady unless you want to."

"Why couldn't you and Mr. Sargent be our lawyers?" asked Hull.

"Well, you see lawyers are not supposed to act for two different people whose interests may be in conflict. The theory of the law is that a lawyer must be free at all times to act for the best interest of his client, and if he acts for two people whose interests are not the same, he is likely to have to choose which one he is going to favor, and no man can serve two masters."

"Who should we get for a lawyer?" asked Tomasi.

We suggested Gelsie Monti. This selection was made because Monti, not long before, had successfully raised the question as to the right of the court to question those who were arrested for intoxication as to the source of the liquor that intoxicated them. This custom had been in vogue in Vermont for more than half a century. Mr. Monti had successfully raised the constitutional issue as appears by the opinion in the case of In Re Harry Dewar (1929) 102 vt. 340. The decision in that case put an end to the fifty-year practice of requiring those convicted of intoxication to disclose by holding the statute unconstitutional. The boys took our suggestion to engage Mr. Monti to look after their interests.

In due course the case of *State* v. *Shady* came on for trial. After appropriate instructions to the jury from the judge, the prosecution got under way. A quick look around the courtroom disclosed that the state, as we had hoped, was going to rely entirely on the testimony of the two boys. Hull was called to the stand first, and, after being asked a few preliminary questions, such as his name and address, the state's attorney directed the attention of the witness to the occasion in question and asked if he had purchased liquor from Mrs. Shady on that date.

This was the crucial point. Up until that time it had become well established as a rule of law in Vermont, in the minds of all judges, as well as trial lawyers, that in order to claim the constitutional privilege against testifying to incriminate oneself, the witness must personally claim the privilege. No lawyer was supposed to have a right to claim it for him. It was accordingly the custom in such cases for the lawyer to take the witness aside before the trial and instruct him or her thoroughly and painstakingly in the technical niceties of claiming one's privilege, so as to be sure that the witness would get in all of the elements necessary to make him or her entitled to the privilege. I have no doubt that this duty had been thoroughly and painstakingly performed by

Monti. It remained to be seen whether the instruction had been properly absorbed.

To our great disappointment, it was immediately apparent that Hull had not fully mastered his lesson. He attempted in his own embarrassed and futile way to let the court know that he did not wish to testify. When questioned as to why he did not propose to testify, there was a long and embarrassing silence. After considerable prodding, the boy mumbled something about the Constitution, but, try as he would, he was unable to put into clear and appropriate words the fact that the reason for his refusal was that it was his desire to avoid incrimination by claiming the privilege afforded by the Constitution.

At this point Judge Scott took a hand. With a stern expression he looked poor Hull straight in the eye and said, "Do you mean to tell us that, if you testify in answer to this question, it will show you are guilty of a crime?" Startled and confused, the boy answered, "Oh, no." The judge settled back in his seat and ordered Hull to answer the pending question. At this point Monti arose with great dignity and addressed the court. He told the judge that he was there as counsel for Hull; that Hull had explained to him that he wished to claim his privilege; that it was manifest that this was what he was trying to do; and that it was the duty of the court, under the circumstances, to grant the boy's request.

Judge Scott persisted in his ruling. Monti persisted in his argument. Then Judge Scott lost his patience and ordered Monti to sit down. Monti refused to sit down. Thereupon Judge Scott ordered the court officer to escort Monti from the courtroom to prevent him from further obstructing justice. The officer complied. As Monti was being cheerfully escorted from the courtroom, he turned around and addressed his client and told him to stick to his position and refuse to testify. Surprisingly enough, the boy had the necessary courage to do so, and as the questions proceeded he stated flatly that he would not answer any questions, and moreover he would not give any reason why he would not testify. Thereupon the judge ordered the court officer to take the boy into custody, to take him downstairs, and lock him up in jail for contempt of court. Hull left the room in the custody of the officer.

Then Tomasi was asked to take the stand, and, after testifying to a few preliminary questions, he was likewise asked if on the night in question he had purchased liquor from Mrs. Shady. As a witness, he was perhaps even worse than Hull. Judge Scott repeated the question that he had asked of Hull, as to whether the answer to the pending question would tend to show him guilty of a crime. Tomasi answered, "I don't know." The judge ordered him to answer the pending question. Monti, in the meantime, after having been escorted from the courtroom, had apparently walked around through the corridor, had entered the courtroom through a side door from the judge's private office, and had come into the courtroom unobserved by anybody. At this point in the proceedings Monti rose again in defense of his second client. He repeated the argument that he had made for Hull.

Judge Scott persisted in his ruling, and Monti persisted in his argument. Again the judge ordered the officer to remove Monti from the courtroom. By this time the jury was getting great enjoyment out of the tableau and showed it by loud laughter. As he left the room Monti repeated to Tomasi the same admonitory instructions that he had previously given to the same effect to Hull, instructing him to stick to his guns and refuse to testify. His courage bolstered by Hull's refusal, Tomasi likewise refused flatly to answer a single question. He was promptly ordered into custody and locked up in jail with Hull.

The judge ordered that the trial proceed. Unfortunately, the trial couldn't proceed because there were no more witnesses. The state's attorney explained the situation to the judge, and, while the judge was considering what should be done, Sargent arose and made a motion for a directed verdict of acquittal for lack of evidence to sustain the charge against Mrs. Shady. This motion was promptly and unceremoniously denied, and the judge ordered that a continuance of the case be noted on the records and that the jury be discharged to await what might happen.

Monti, with amazing foresight, had prepared petitions for writs of habeas corpus for each of his two clients, which he apparently had in his pocket during the proceedings in court. After his second exit from the courtroom, he drove immediately to Montpelier and presented the petitions to the Honorable Leighton P. Slack, a justice of the Supreme Court. After considering the petitions, Justice Slack signed the writs, which ordered and directed the chief of police to bring the two boys before him. Justice Slack then ordered that bail be fixed for the later appearance of the witnesses, and after bail was furnished they were released. The justice, in accordance with a practice that is quite common, adjourned the two cases into Supreme Court so that the full bench might pass on the questions presented. In due course the cases were briefed and argued in the Supreme Court.

At the next term judgments were handed down holding that Hull and Tomasi were illegally deprived of their liberty and should be released. The opinion cut through the technicalities that had been gradually built up by interpretation during the historical evolution of the subject. And with a refreshing logic and directness it pointed out that the constitutional guarantee was so basic and important in our jurisprudence that it was not to be denied because of the inability of a witness to understand the niceties of the method of properly claiming his privilege on the stand.

The court held, in effect, that the right was so sacred that it was the duty of the judge to lean over backwards to help the witness claim the privilege where, as here, it was obvious that the witness did not wish to testify, and that to require him to do so would clearly have the effect of forcing him to give evidence against himself that would tend to show him guilty of a crime.

Thus was struck another blow for freedom.

Lawyers or Liars?

My father was a country lawyer as was I. He preferred male secretaries over females, for reasons that were never clear to me. A number of young men later became successful lawyers as a result of becoming interested in the law while serving as secretary in my father's office. Among them were Gelsie Monti of Barre City and Ugo J. A. Carusi, formerly of Barre, who had a distinguished career on a national basis. Ugo was assistant to the Vermont attorney general, served as executive assistant to five U.S. attorneys general after being taken to Washington by U.S. attorney general John Sargent. Later he became U.S. commissioner of immigration.

Ugo's parents were immigrants who came from Italy to Barre, where his father worked in the granite sheds. He died at an early age. Ugo began his work for my father when he was still in short pants in Spaulding High School in Barre. His salary was the munificent sum of two dollars per week. He was supposed to work during the afternoons after each high school session ended for the day.

Shortly after the arrangement had been made for his employment between Ugo and my father and before Ugo had actually started work, my father was working late one night in his office when he heard a noise in the outer office and went out to investigate. He found his visitor to be an Italian lady with the traditional Italian shawl over her head and an interested, inquiring expression on her face. My father asked the lady what, if anything, he could do for her.

"You Mr. Davees?"

"Yes, I am," replied my father. "What can I do for you?"

"You hire-a my boy?"

"Oh, you must be Ugo's mother. Are you Ugo's mother? Yes, I did hire him. And I hope you approve."

"Yes, Mr. Davees, I think I approve. But," she asked, with a searching glance straight into my father's eyes, "you wonn-a teach-a him to lie, will-a you, Mr. Davees?"

A Bit of a Shock

In the early days of my practice, bastardy cases were much more numerous than at present. Why, I do not know. In fact, in rural Vermont cases were sufficiently frequent to produce a sort of "going rate" for voluntary settlement, and a large proportion of these cases was settled out of court. It was very difficult to defend a bastardy case once the father was named by the young lady in question. Hence, in those early days the expression was frequently heard that "in Republican Primaries and bastardy cases nomination is equivalent to election." And so a sort of average "market price" was developed, which then was $300. In retrospect it seems almost incredible that the going price could be as low as $300, even giving due weight to inflation.

On one occasion the sheriff of Essex County went to serve a body writ on a young man charged with being the father of a child born to an unmarried girl. When the sheriff arrived at the home of the parents of the accused, armed with his writ, consternation broke out. "What can we do about it?" inquired the alarmed father of the accused. "Well, you've got three alternatives," replied the sheriff. "First, you can pay my fees and $300 and that will settle the matter. If you don't want to do that, you can pay me my fees and have him marry the girl, and that will settle it. And if you don't want to do that, you can pay my fees and I'll take the boy down and lock him up in Guildhall jail.''

I had my share of these cases, which were considered by the lawyers as sort of routine, run-of-the-mill business. One day a woman from an adjoining town came to my office with her 16-year-old daughter. It seemed that her daughter "had loved not wisely but too well.'' But the unusual thing about the interview was that the mother did all the talking. Although I addressed my questions to the daughter, invariably the daughter would turn and look at her mother, and promptly the mother would give the answer. It almost seemed as though she must have been "there.'' She knew when *it* happened, where *it* happened, how *it* happened, why *it* happened, and by whom *it* happened. She even knew when the baby was going to be born and confidently fixed the date of birth to be between February 1 and February 5 next. Another thing that startled me about the interview was that she named a prominent man of the town as the father.

I found the story a little difficult to believe. And so, in my youth and innocence, I decided that here discretion was the better part of valor. "Mrs. Sargent,'' I said, "under our law the case couldn't be tried until the baby is born. So we won't issue a writ until the baby is born. You take Ethel home, and right after the baby is born you let me know and *I'll see what I can do about it.*''

During the second week in February a letter came to the office from Mrs. Sargent. My secretary opened it, read it, brought it into my room, and laid it down on my desk. She said nothing as she turned and left the room, but I noticed that she had a broad grin on her face. I picked up the letter and looked at it. It was written on coarse brown wrapping paper, and the handwriting ran kitty-corner across the paper. This is what it said:

Dear Mr. Davis: Ethel's baby was born last Saturday. What are you going to do about it?

Evenhanded Justice

During the early years of my law practice a surprisingly large number of legal disputes were tried before justices of the peace. At that time there were 1,700 justices of the peace in the state, appointed by the governor. All of them had certain judicial powers and jurisdiction. Many of them occasionally exercised these powers, and a few exercised them rather frequently and gradually earned the reputation of being a judge. Their jurisdiction was quite limited. They had final jurisdiction in civil cases on the facts in cases under twenty dollars. They had preliminary jurisdiction in civil cases up to two hundred dollars, which meant that these cases could be appealed to County Court and retried de novo there. They also had jurisdiction to try misdemeanors and to hold hearings for binding over proceedings in felonies.

Justices were empowered by statute to impanel a jury of six persons upon application of either party in civil cases. But in many cases they found the facts themselves without the aid of a jury. Many of these justices gradually picked up a surprising fund of knowledge in some of the more common and basic provisions of the law. And what they lacked in more advanced knowledge of the law they made up for in a remarkable fund of common sense.

In the early 1920's, John Palmer was driving his Ford touring car through the main street of East Corinth Village. As the car was about to pass Frank Simpson's house, Frank's prize Rhode Island Red rooster suddenly ran across the road in front of the approaching car, with disastrous consequences to the rooster and some damage to the automobile. The impact brought instant demise to the rooster and put a sizable dent in John's radiator, from which boiling water and steam emerged in copious quantity.

In those days "lawing" before justices of the peace was one way of paying off grudges. Such cases had the added social value of providing good entertainment for the townspeople in remote rural areas who were deprived of other forms of entertainment. The amount of money involved was quite unimportant. It was always the "principle" involved.

Bad blood between Palmer and Simpson had existed for years and was a matter of general knowledge locally. At the scene of the accident a violent argument broke out between Simpson and Palmer, which was not settled satisfactorily to either party.

In a few days Simpson was served with a summons to appear before the local justice of the peace to answer to a claim for damages for negligence in operating a motor vehicle resulting in the death of one valuable Rhode Island Red rooster of the value of ten dollars. In due course the trial commenced by counsel, and a six-man jury was impaneled. The Town Hall, where the trial was held, was filled to capacity with town citizens, who correctly anticipated a good show.

As a model of trial procedure it was a complete loss. But as a drama of small-town background it was a howling success. The townspeople received their full money's worth. After four hours of public display of the animosities between Simpson and Palmer, very little of which had anything to do with the facts surrounding the accident, the jury was instructed by Justice Hammond to retire to an anteroom to consider its verdict.

After several hours of waiting while the jury deliberated, the spectators were rewarded by the return of the jury to the hall. The judge called the court to order and addressed the foreman of the jury as follows:

"Mr. Foreman, and gentlemen of the jury, have you agreed upon a verdict?"

"We have, Your Honor."

"What is your verdict, Mr. Foreman?"

"We have it here in writing, Your Honor."

"Let me have your verdict," directed Justice Hammond. The foreman handed over a paper, which the justice read silently to himself with a most puzzled expression on his face. The puzzled expression continued, during which the interest of the spectators rose to a new height. Finally, Justice Hammond read the verdict to the people in the courtroom as follows:

> We, the jury, hereby decide that John Palmer drove his car too fast, so he should pay for the rooster. We also decide that Frank Simpson should have kept his rooster to home, so he should pay for fixing the radiator. We therefore decide that Frank owes John a net sum of five dollars, and that each party should pay his own court costs.

An Honest Liar

One of the interesting studies in human nature is the extent to which testimony in court may be influenced by the power of suggestion. The successful trial lawyer soon comes to understand and appreciate this phenomenon and to learn how to use it in the examination and cross-examination of witnesses. When a witness testifies to something he or she has seen or heard, the witness is of course supposed to testify only to that which his or her memory recalls as a visual or auditory impression. The power of suggestion is used to stimulate the act of memory. But, more than that, the power of suggestion can be, and frequently is, used to conjure up in the mind of the witness an impression of a fact or event that never happened. In many instances witnesses will testify to such facts or events with complete honesty. The visual or auditory impression is entirely real to them and often more clear and definite than the mental image of events that actually happened.

When this phenomenon occurs it is usually the result of the converging influence of three different stimuli: the power of suggestion, the seeming reasonableness and naturalness of the fact or event suggested, and the existence on the part of the witness of a desire to have the particular fact appear. In the hands of a skillful trier this power of suggestion can be used in cross-examination to test the truth of testimony of adverse witnesses. The following illustration indicates how easily a perfectly honest person can be misled to believe and testify to an event that never happened.

Josiah Fuller was a learned and skillful lawyer who practiced his profession in one of the larger counties of Vermont. Were it not for his addiction to the use of alcohol, he would have been one of the leading lawyers of the state during his generation. As it was, he was recognized by his brothers at the bar as one of the most skillful men of his time to dictate trial strategy, and he was often called in by other lawyers to help carry the load of a difficult case.

Josiah's father, the Reverend Horace Fuller, was a Congregationalist minister, and he was proud of all of his five children except his lawyer son. Perhaps the parson could have overlooked his son's being a lawyer, but he could not forgive his use of liquor, and so it came generally to be known that the parson regarded Josiah as the black sheep of the family. Not surprisingly, when the parson came late in life to make his will, Josiah was cut off with a dollar, and all of the parson's modest estate was directed to be divided equally among his four other children.

After the parson's death, Josiah's sister, Mary, discovered the parson's will in the family safe. Not knowing what to do with it, she brought it to her lawyer brother, Josiah. He opened it and, of course, discovered that it was his father's wish and direction that he, Josiah, should be cut off with a dollar. But he discovered more. The names of only two witnesses appeared as attesting witnesses, and Josiah knew that the law of Vermont required three in order that the document be valid as a will. He also knew, of course, that if the will was invalid, then the parson's estate would be divided among his next of kin which in this case would be the five children, including Josiah. But Josiah had a high sense of honor. In fact, he felt that it was his duty to see that his father's wishes were carried out even if he had to commit forgery to do it, even if the effect of that forgery would be to disinherit himself. So he followed the dictates of his conscience and secretly forged the name of a third witness to the will and filed it in Probate Court for allowance.

The testimony elicited at the hearing on the allowance of the will is a fine lesson in psychology and shows how well Josiah understood human nature and the workings of the human mind, particularly in the witness chair.

The two witnesses whose names were actually signed to the will were John Adams, a local banker, and Dr. William Graves, the parson's physician, both of whom were close friends of the parson. The parson had another close friend, one Thomas Jones, who for years had shared the only real hobby in which the parson indulged himself. They were fishing devotees. It was the name of Thomas Jones that Josiah added to the will, and the selection was made after due deliberation and with a view to effecting exactly the evidential sequence that followed.

Where there is no contest of the allowance of a will, the law permits the due execution of a will to be proved by the testimony of only one of the attesting witnesses. After the necessary publication of notice in the newspaper, the matter came on for hearing before the Probate Judge of the District. Josiah was present in court with Adams as his only witness to the due execution of the will. I suspect that he selected Adams rather than Graves because, in the circumstances, it would give him a certain amount of pleasure to make an unconscious liar out of the man he intensely disliked because he was so pious in bearing and mien. Adams was a pillar of the parson's church and fancied himself as a man of piety and honor. He had helped to influence the parson to disown his son.

Adams was sworn by the judge to "tell the whole truth and nothing but the truth." The expression on Adams's face as he took the oath showed quite clearly that he regarded the oath as a wholly unnecessary insult and that it was inconceivable that anyone should think that the circumstances required an oath from him in order to get the truth. Obviously, he felt that his well-known reputation for honesty and stability as a banker and churchman should be assurance to anyone that he would cut off his right arm before he would deviate a hair's breadth from the absolute truth. The examination proceeded with Josiah asking the questions.

"Were you acquainted with my father, the Reverend Horace Fuller, during his lifetime?"

"Yes, sir, well acquainted. We were close friends."

"At some time were you asked to witness the execution of his last will and testament?"

"I was."

"When was this?"

"I don't recall the exact date, but it was about a year and a half ago."

"I show you a paper that purports to be the last will and testament of my father. Will you refresh your recollection by observation of that paper, and tell us when it was that you attended the execution of my father's will?"

"Yes, sir," said Adams, looking at the date on the will, it was January 16, year before last."

"Calling your attention to the signature at the lower right-hand corner of this paper, can you tell us whose signature that is?"

"That is the signature of your father," said Adams, clearly showing by his expression that he thought it was unnecessary to ask.

"Were you present when his name was signed?"

"I was."

"Were others present?"

"Yes, sir."

"Who else was present?" asked Josiah, again handing the will to the witness with the subtle invitation that he look at it.

Adams glanced at the names appearing as witnesses and promptly and definitely answered, "William Graves and Thomas Jones."

"Do you know how Dr. Graves and Thomas Jones happened to be there?"

"Well, your father asked me to come over to the house and witness his will, and the doctor was there because he was sick at the time. I told your father that we needed a third witness, and so he sent for Tom to come over."

"Were all three of you present when father signed this paper?"

"Yes, sir."

"Did you see both Graves and Jones sign their names on that occasion?"

"Oh, yes."

And so with complete honesty did Adams testify to a complete falsehood. The power of suggestion, the reasonableness of the fact suggested, and the desire to see the will validated concurred to create the image of an incident that never happened.

Too Little Evidence

During the days of National Prohibition, I served a term of office as grand juror of the City of Barre and later a term as state's attorney of Washington County. Hence, during that period, a substantial portion of my time was necessarily devoted to the investigation and prosecution of complaints for illegal possession or sales of intoxicating liquors under the Volstead Act. An active chapter of the Women's Christian Temperance Society was alert and vigilant to insure that no prosecuting officer did less than his full duty.

On one occasion the Barre City Police made a raid on a household in Barre commonly known as being engaged in "the business." When the officers entered the kitchen there were two gallon jugs of whiskey sitting on a shelf beside the sink. The minute the officers appeared the lady of the house smashed both jugs in the sink and the contents ran down the drain. Seated at the kitchen table was a customer, Ed Rogers, with a glass and a quart bottle in which there remained a small quantity of whiskey, perhaps a glassful or so. The police sequestered the bottle, but a thorough search of the rest of the premises disclosed no more liquor.

Eventually the case came to trial in Barre City Municipal Court on this very thin bit of evidence. Juries in those days were nearly always loath to convict in liquor cases and only needed an excuse, sometimes pretty thin, in order to acquit. So the desperate nature of the case was quite clear to me as official prosecutor.

Rogers was on the stand. He testified that he had not drunk anything before the officers arrived. And, of course, there was no way to dispute that. But he did admit the presence of the whiskey bottle on the table at which he was sitting. It was also quite evident from his attitude that he was not about to help the state in any way if he could avoid committing perjury—a not unnatural attitude under the circumstances.

Asked if he knew what the bottle contained, he replied in the negative. My only hope of conviction was to prove "possession" by the respondent. And that necessitated proving that the liquid in the bottle was intoxicating liquor.

"Mr. Rogers, I now show you a bottle marked for identification State's Exhibit A, containing a quantity of fluid. Have you seen this bottle before?"

"Yes sir," he answered.

"Where did you see it?"

"It was on the table in the kitchen when the officers arrived."

"Very well, Mr. Rogers, I now hand you the bottle and ask that you look at it, smell of the contents, and, if necessary, taste it and tell this jury whether it contains intoxicating liquor."

He took the bottle, looked at it for several moments, removed the cork and smelled of the contents, still with an innocent but very doubtful look on his face. Then he carefully raised the bottle to his lips. Too late, now, I realized that I

had committed a stupid error by inviting him to taste it. I watched with horror and the jury watched with amusement as the very last drop of the whiskey gurgled down his throat. He slowly handed the bottle back to me and with a most serious expression on his face replied, "I just can't be sure."

Verdict: not guilty.

A Mitigating Circumstance

One of the most colorful members of the Vermont judiciary was the late Honorable Harland B. Howe, who for many years presided over the Federal District Court of Vermont. In those days we had only one federal judge for the district instead of two as we do now. A trial conducted before Judge Howe, with or without jury, was never a dull affair. If the case itself lacked entertainment value, he was prone to supply it himself, and he was an expert entertainer.

The judge was an ardent Democrat at a time when the Democrats were not only a minority party in Vermont but a very small minority at that. He took a keen interest in political matters, although judges are expected to withdraw from political matters upon ascending the bench. And he had great influence. He was a prolific and convincing letter writer, and, when he was aroused, he was an influence to be reckoned with.

He had a strong feeling for the underdog and never tried to hide that feeling in the courtroom. He could influence a jury from the bench about as skillfully and effectively as any judge I ever knew. Lawyers and the public tolerated this modest breach of legal impartiality because of his essential honesty and also, I suppose, because he was such a colorful personality.

His sympathy for the underdog was in part an inherited characteristic but was greatly strengthened by the circumstances of his practice in Caledonia as a young lawyer. In those days there were many cases against the railroads of Vermont. And Caledonia was no exception. Judge Howe found himself in those days representing claimants, and usually claimants in impecunious circumstances. When plaintiffs won, the railroads usually took the cases to the Supreme Court on appeal, and this was a long and expensive procedure for his clients.

Years later, when Lawyer Howe had become the judge of the District Court following World War I, much of the time of his court was taken up with suits against the government for compensation for service-connected disabilities under a statute passed by Congress. The question of whether the disability was "service-connected" was a difficult and complex one to determine in the majority of the cases, as also was the measurement of the extent of the disability.

I remember watching him trying some of these cases. His sympathies were always with the service person. Again and again in ruling on evidence or motions he would refer to the plaintiff as a "soldier boy." "Remember," he would say, discussing the admissibility of evidence, "we're dealing here with a soldier boy, a soldier boy who was serving his country." And the timbre of his voice and the subtle intonation invariably conjured up visions of sacrifice and patriotism that struck responsive chords in the hearts of jurors in those days, when patriotism was still considered a virtue. Expressions like these often repeated during the trial would usually, by their cumulative effect, assure a verdict for the plaintiff "soldier boy."

And the judge was a fighter by nature. I feel sure that he must have enjoyed his years as a trial lawyer more than his years on the bench. Once during the later years of his service on the bench, I was riding on the train from Montpelier to Brattleboro where I was to hold court in the County Court in Newfane. He was traveling to Brattleboro to hold a term of District Court in the Federal District Court there. We sat together. He said to me, "You know, Judge, I'm about ready to give up this judging business. You know, just as soon as I can be sure of getting a Democrat appointed in my place, and just as soon as I can get up courage, and as soon as I can get my wife's consent, I'm going to give up this judging business, and I'm going back to practicing law. And I'm going to be a fighting lawyer, not one of those d—— settling lawyers!"

Another strong prejudice of his was his hatred of Prohibition. During the years of Prohibition his court was busy with liquor cases based on the famous Volstead Act, which made it illegal to possess, transport, or sell intoxicating liquors. Watching him perform in these liquor cases was great fun.

Vermont was geographically a natural corridor from Canada to Massachusetts and other lower New England States and to the New York City area and New Jersey. And the remote uninhabited character of the terrain at the Vermont-Canadian border made it easy for the rumrunners to outwit the officers who tried to catch them. So an extensive and lucrative business of transporting liquor from Canada, where it was legal, to and through Vermont grew up in those years. When some did get caught, they wound up in Judge Howe's court. The judge always tried to help the respondent in these cases, not because he regarded the rumrunners as underdogs but, rather, because he thought the Volstead Act a mistake and he hated it. But, if, in spite of his efforts, a respondent was found guilty by the jury, the judge's sentence was inclined to be pretty severe. His feeling was that, if the sentence was severe, it would bring public reaction against the Volstead Act and expedite its repeal, as he always prophesied.

Occasionally the judge would be called to assist in the District Court that included the City of New York, where there was always a heavy docket during the days of Prohibition. His sessions were always crowded with spectators as soon as word got around that Judge Howe was presiding.

On one occasion, so the story goes, the judge was on his way out of the courthouse at noon recess on his way to lunch when he met one of the other judges coming up the steps. He was warmly greeted. Then he was asked, "How you getting along, Judge?" "Oh fine," he answered. "We got four of 'em off this morning, but I'm afraid they're going to beat us this afternoon."

The judge did believe that lawyers who defended these rumrunners should be well paid. He recognized that theirs was a lucrative business. One of these respondents, caught with a car loaded with liquor near the Canadian border, wound up in Judge Howe's court charged with illegal transportation. The respondent pleaded guilty. The prosecuting officer was the late Allen Martin, district attorney. The respondent was not represented by counsel. Noting the absence of counsel, which always offended the judge, he asked the respondent, "Where is your lawyer?"

"I haven't got a lawyer, your honor."

"Why haven't you got a lawyer?" asked the judge.

"Because I can't afford it and I don't think I need one."

"Oh!" said the judge, "well, all right. If you haven't got interest enough in your case to have a lawyer to see if there is some mitigating circumstance bearing on sentence, then I'll just have to assume there are no mitigating circumstances. So, Mr. Clerk, I guess you'll just have to enter up judgment of guilty in this case and I guess a sentence of, well I guess the maximum, a year and a day in jail."

The respondent's interest heightened immediately.

"Well, just a minute, your honor, maybe if you could give me just a little time I could find a lawyer."

"All right. You go ahead and find a lawyer, and we'll go on with the other business."

So the respondent went out to the telephone and called Arthur Theriault, then a well-known lawyer practicing in Montpelier whose office was near the courthouse. Theriault agreed to come over and give what assistance he could. After looking over the case and seeing that there was no defense to the charge, Theriault and his client came back into court.

"Oh," said the judge, "I see you have a lawyer."

"Yes, your honor."

"All right, Mr. Theriault," said the judge, "now, let's see. Have you got the money for your fee?"

"No," said Theriault.

"Why haven't you got your money? You know you can't trust these rumrunners."

"Well, there isn't much I can do for this man anyway, your honor, but I thought we'd get the case over with and then we'd adjust the fee."

"No, no, I won't hear you. You take this man out into the lawyer's room and get an appropriate fee."

So Theriault and his client repaired again to the lawyer's room and, after some discussion, returned.

"Well, did you get your fee, Mr. Theriault?"

"Yes, your honor, I did."

"How much?"

"Fifty dollars."

"Fifty dollars!" said the judge. "No, no. It's a disgrace to the bar. No, I won't hear you. Take him back out and get a decent fee."

So, once again out went Theriault and his client. Soon they came back, ready to proceed further.

"All right now, Mr. Theriault, did you get your fee?"

"Yes, your honor, I did."

"How much did you get?"

"I got a hundred dollars."

"Ridiculous! A hundred dollars! Why, that's a disgrace, Mr. Theriault. But we can't waste the time of the court any more. You really ought to be disbarred for downgrading the profession. But we'll hear you. Now you've got the hundred dollars, Mr. Theriault, let's see you start earning that hundred dollars. Can you tell me of a mitigating circumstance that would bear on the sentence of this respondent?"

"Yes, your honor. When this man was arrested he was placed under cash bail of $500, and when the case came up last March he was not located in time; and so on a technicality the bail was forfeited, and he has already lost $500."

"Oh," said the judge, "Bail jumper, is he? Well, you know, I was going to fine him about $100 and costs, but I guess now, being a bail jumper, I'll have to raise that to about $300 and costs."

"Well, just a minute, your honor. There's another mitigating circumstance."

"Well, what's that?"

"Well, you know, he brought this liquor in from Canada in a brand new Packard car that cost him $2,000. And the government forfeited his car under the statute."

"Oh," said the judge, "you know they couldn't forfeit his car unless this was a commercial transaction. Yes, commercial transaction. Well now, I was going to fine him about

$300 and costs. I guess I'll have to fine him about $750 and costs. Now have you got any more mitigating circumstances, Mr. Theriault?''

Who Said?

My perennial client, Walter Bixby, of East Barre, was what was known in the Vermont vernacular as a horse jockey—not one who rode horses in races, as the term is generally used, but one who makes a living trading horses. Walt would trade anything. His customary greeting when he dropped into my office, which he so frequently did, was, "Do you know where I could go today to make an honest dollar?"

One day, as a result of one of his trades, he brought me a note for collection. It involved the sale of a yearling Guernsey bull and was in the principal sum of seventy-five dollars. It seemed that the purchaser of the bull, Lucien Couillard, had refused to pay because, as he claimed, Walt had guaranteed that the bull could be registered in the Guernsey Breed Association Registry, which of course meant that he was purebred, not crossbred. He had to be the progeny of parents that were registered on both sides in the registry.

"Did you warrant that the bull could be registered?" I asked Walt.

"No, I didn't," said Walt. "Mr. Trombley, the man I bought the bull from, said he could be registered."

Here is how the note read:

For Value received, I hereby promise to pay to Walter Bixby the sum of Seventy-Five Dollars without interest. Payable to him or his order sixty days after this date. This note is given for one yearling Guernsey Bull, known as the Trombley Bull. He says can be registered.

Lucien Couillard

The case came up for trial in the Municipal Court of Barre City amid much hilarity. The issue was to whom did the word *he* refer—Bixby, Couillard, Trombley or the bull. The jury decided that it was Trombley.

Who Won?

The law of Vermont formerly provided that when an indigent person became a town charge the town where he actually was at the time he needed assistance should be originally liable to furnish the assistance. But the law also provided that such town could recover from the town where the indigent person had last resided "for three years supporting himself and family." Simple as this wording seems, it became the cause of many bitter controversies between towns respecting which town was the proper one to be charged with the support of the indigent person.

In one case Eph Perrin became a charge on the Town of Calais, since he was living there when he needed assistance. But he had also lived at various times in the adjoining town of East Montpelier. Being somewhat of a gypsy at heart and in action, it became a complicated question of fact as to whether he had actually resided in East Montpelier for three years "supporting himself and family" at a prior time.

The case was tried by jury in County Court at Montpelier and lasted for several days. It became the chief conversation piece at Haskell's country store each evening. Each day Eph hitchhiked to Montpelier to watch the trial of his case and hitchhiked back each night when court adjourned for the day. The hangers-on at the store waited eagerly each evening for Eph's arrival back in Calais to give a blow-by-blow description of what had transpired during the day.

Finally, the day came when everybody knew that a verdict would be rendered. Eph was late getting back to the country store, and when he walked in the air was thick with dramatic suspense. As he came through the door and saw the eager countenances of the hangers-on, he announced the result with great flourish:

"Calais won! Calais got me!"

Justice by Technicality

The manner in which a person may pass property by will is prescribed by statute in each state. Certain formalities must be followed to the letter, or the will is held to be invalid. These formal requirements sometimes work a hardship or even injustice, where the formalities are not followed because of ignorance or accident.

These occasional instances of disallowance of wills for what may appear to be technical reasons have caused criticism of the law for what has been characterized as undue rigidity and "worship of form." But, with the law as with people, it is so much easier to see and condemn the bad than it is to recognize and applaud the good. Experience has shown that, where the requirement of certain formalities surrounding the execution of wills was not in existence, many frauds were being practiced. These formalities first were prescribed in England by the Statute of Wills, and from this original act have stemmed all of the statutes of the American states, which, although not all identical, have a common inheritance and are in substance similar.

Thus the law of Vermont requires, among other things,

that a will be in writing and witnessed by three persons who must all be in the presence of the testator when he or she signs and who must sign in each other's presence. It is the theory of the law that these formalities and the presence of a number of witnesses are a safeguard against the exercise of undue influence by designing persons and also a protection against the fraudulent proof of spurious documents as the will of a person.

Hiram Atwood was a respected resident of the Town of Tunbridge, where he had lived and carried on a farm for most of his adult life. He had been married and brought up a family of three children, all of whom had ultimately left Vermont and established themselves in useful occupations. Hiram had lost his wife and had reached the ripe old age of eighty years, and he was suffering from physical disabilities that required the attention of someone to live with him and minister to his needs. His children tried to get him to leave Vermont and come to live with one of them, but he loved his home and he loved Vermont, and he steadfastly refused to leave.

He had accumulated a fairly sizable sum of money that made him financially independent, and he very definitely intended to be wholly self-sufficient. The children insisted that he should find a suitable housekeeper who could do domestic nursing, and finally Hiram yielded to their persuasions and advertised in the *New England Homestead* for such a person. In due time he received an answer to his ad from a woman who lived near Glens Falls, New York. After an exchange of correspondence, the applicant, a Mrs. Nichols, presented herself for an interview and was hired. This event pleased the children, who now felt that their father's health, comfort, and safety were provided for.

Mrs. Nichols was a married woman whose husband was employed in a garage in Glens Falls, and he continued to live in Glens Falls, making occasional trips to Tunbridge to visit his wife. She was an excellent housekeeper and was diligent in looking after the comforts of her employer. But Hiram began to fail, and at times his mind was very weak. As Mrs. Nichols became aware of the size of his bank accounts she became more diligent in her efforts to please Hiram, and gradually she ingratiated herself to him to such an extent that she could influence him to do anything she desired. Finally, she persuaded Hiram to make a will leaving all of his property to her. Fearing that if a local lawyer were employed to make the will the townspeople might discover that she had influenced him, she arranged with her brother, a lawyer practicing in Albany, to come over and make the will. She arranged with her brother to bring his secretary with him and also Mrs. Nichols's husband to act as the witnesses to the will. This witnessing would obviate the necessity of asking any of the townspeople to attend the execution of the will and would keep entirely secret the fact that a will had been made. So in due course the will was made and signed, and the three witnesses were the lawyer, his secretary, and Mrs. Nichols's husband.

About a year later Hiram died. After the funeral Mrs. Nichols produced the will and read it to the three children. They were quite shocked to learn that their father's entire life savings were to go to this woman, a comparative stranger, and they may perhaps be forgiven if they expressed their disappointment by upbraiding Mrs. Nichols in rather choice language. But, as far as they could see, nothing could be done about it now, and so they returned to their homes. Mrs. Nichols promptly filed the will in the Probate Court at Chelsea, and, in accordance with the mandate of the statute, notice of a hearing on the allowance of the will was published for three weeks in a newspaper circulating in the vicinity.

One of the children was a schoolteacher who lived in New Jersey. She could not reconcile herself to the fact that all of this property was to go outside the family and finally persuaded herself that something must be done about the situation. A few days before the date of the hearing she came to Chelsea to consult a local lawyer who had been a schoolmate of hers. He agreed to represent her interests.

On the day of the hearing Mrs. Nichols appeared in court with her brother, the New York lawyer, and also her husband. The brother and Mr. Nichols both testified in detail to the execution of the will and then rested their case. Whereupon counsel for the schoolteacher arose and addressed the probate judge:

> Your Honor, on behalf of the legal heirs and next of kin of the testator I desire at this time to move that the court enter an order that the entire legacy to Mrs. Nichols be declared null and void. It has appeared in evidence that Mr. George Nichols, one of the attesting witnesses, is the husband of Mrs. Nichols, the legatee. Section 2755 P.L. of Vermont provides as follows, and I read it verbatim: "If a person, other than an heir at law, attests the execution of a will, to whom, or to whose wife or husband, a beneficial devise, legacy or interest...is given by such will, such devise, legacy or interest shall, so far only as concerns such person, or the wife or husband of such person...be void.

Now it was Mrs. Nichols's turn to be shocked. She looked at her lawyer brother, he looked at the judge, and the judge looked quite pleased. He had known Hiram well for many years and no doubt had his own ideas of what was justice in this case.

"That is the law in Vermont," he said. "It may not be the

law elsewhere, but it's the law here all right. It is my duty to declare the legacy void, and, because there are no other provisions in the will, the whole estate will be decreed in equal parts to the children of Hiram Atwood.''

A Fitting Fact

As a law student in my father's office I was slowly picking up disconnected and unrelated bits of information about the law and its workings. In this way one learns much practical knowledge that cannot be gained from books. One learns that a certain set of facts gives rise to a certain legal result. But this way of learning about the law has its dangers. The theory of the law is important, too, and in this kind of office study there is danger that theory and history and the reason behind the law may be too much neglected.

While my father was away for a few days on a business trip, I was in sole charge of the office. I felt quite important as I boldly dispensed legal advice to unfortunate callers with a degree of confidence that makes me shudder as I recall the events after years of sobering experience.

One of the callers was an elderly man who had just been released from the hospital where he had been undergoing treatment for injuries received in an automobile accident. He was a resident of Massachusetts who had been driving through Vermont with his wife while on vacation. As he was approaching the village of South Barre on the main highway in the town of Barre, he rounded a slight curve and suddenly one wheel of his Model T Ford dropped into a hole in the gravel roadbed. The result was quite disastrous. The steering wheel was snatched out of his hands, and the car turned over twice and came to rest against a fence at the foot of a small embankment. The car was demolished, and Mr. Moore, the driver, as well as his wife who was with him, received substantial injuries.

I had been reading the law of negligence, and some of it was quite fresh in my mind. Moreover, I had watched the progress of several automobile negligence cases through the office and felt quite competent to give advice on a matter of this seeming simplicity. So I explained that my father was away but that I would be glad to convey the matter to him when he returned. I told Moore that it was a clear case of liability on the part of the town to pay the full damages to the car and also for the injuries to himself and his wife. I explained to him that my father would be informed of the details upon his return, and claim would be presented to the town, and, if payment was not promptly made, suit would be brought promptly. Moore left the office to return to his home in Massachusetts.

When my father returned I made a report of the matter and was somewhat disappointed that he did not display a proper amount of gratitude for the service I had rendered in holding such a good case for the office.

"What caused this hole to develop?" he asked.

"Oh, I don't know about that. It was just there."

"Was there any bridge near the point?"

"No."

"Was there a culvert?"

"No. It was just a hole in the middle of the road."

"What did you tell Mr. Moore about liability?" he asked.

"Why, I told him the town was liable, of course."

"What made you think the town was liable?"

"Liable? Of course they're liable. Clear case of negligence. The town has the duty to use reasonable care to keep the road in repair. They allowed this hole over three feet wide and a foot deep to remain right in the middle of the main highway. That's failure to exercise due care. There wasn't any contributory negligence on Moore's part. He didn't know the hole was there. Couldn't, because he came around the curve just before he came to the hole. There's a case right here referred to in *Thompson's Negligence.*"

Father looked glum. "Didn't you bother to check the Vermont statutes before you gave this advice? We have a special statute in Vermont on the liability of towns for negligence in maintenance of highways."

He reached for the *General Laws of Vermont*, and, after turning the pages, he put on his glasses and read the terms of the statute. The statute provided in definite words that a town should be liable for damages caused by the insufficiency of a highway *only* where the insufficiency occurred at a bridge or culvert.

"I'll have to write your Mr. Moore and break the news to him that he can't recover damages. Better be thinking up something pretty good that I can say to him to explain why you muffed the ball."

I felt pretty low all the rest of the day. I was still licking my wounded pride when I went to bed that night. I couldn't get the case out of my mind, and neither could I go to sleep. The words of that statute burned themselves into my mind. I never forgot them and could repeat them verbatim for years afterward. Suddenly, in my desperation and my humiliation, a thought struck me. I rose and dressed and slipped quietly out of the house so as not to waken my father. It was after

midnight. Picking up a flashlight in the cellar, I went out to the barn and as quietly as possible backed Dad's Ford out of the barn and drove with great speed to the scene of the accident. I was breathless with anticipation as I got out of the car and approached the spot. The hole had been filled in with stone and gravel, but the spot was easily identified. As I swept the flashlight over both sides of the road my joy was unrestrained. Directly under the spot where this hole had developed *there was a culvert.*

The next morning, as nonchalantly as possible, I told my father of my discovery of the night before. He listened attentively and said nothing for several minutes.

"Some lawyers achieve success by a thorough knowledge of the law. Others achieve success by fitting the facts to what little law they do know. It's better to be in the first group."

The Jury Is Excused

Cross-examination of witnesses is both an art and a science. The science may be acquired by study of its basic principles, but the art is acquired by the combination of natural talent and long practice. Many outstanding legal scholars never acquire it, whereas many mediocre students of the law become masters of the art. Complete success requires a better-than-average understanding of psychology. The examiner must be able to look into the mind and heart of the witness to understand his or her motives, prejudices, interest, and character. Good cross-examination never proceeds without a definite purpose and objective on the part of the examiner. Yet, this rule is more observed in the breach than in the practice. A certain amount of showmanship is usually employed by the best examiners. A jury trial is really drama being written and produced simultaneously. The opinions of jury members and the testimony of witnesses are affected by the moving sweep of emotional forces set in motion by the living drama of which they are a part. The perceptions are sharpened by the clash and conflict, and understanding is often more acute when the intellect is aided by emotion and feeling.

My partner, J. Ward Carver, was one of the ablest jury lawyers of his day. No small part of his success was due to his master showmanship and his great understanding of human nature. To him every trial was a play and, like the great actors, he lived and loved every moment. He was the leading man in every trial in which he was involved. His motions, his gestures, and even the expressions of his countenance were designed to dramatize the essential points of his case. They were instinctive rather than studied, but they were effective. Moreover, he possessed the rare ability to read the expression on the faces of witnesses and members of the jury and thus know what was going on in their minds and hearts. He had a rare instinct, too, that enabled him to gauge the effect on the jurors of evidence before it appeared. He watched the jury and the witnesses like a hawk, even while he was busily engaged in questioning witnesses or arguing motions before the judge. The most routine case had great entertainment value when he was one of counsel.

Yet, with the most careful planning and skillful execution on the part of the cross-examiner it is surprising how often the result is pure accident.

Fred Gleason and I were defending a murder case during the trial of which occurred an incident that illustrates this fact. The respondent, Joseph Pironi, had been charged with the murder of Emilio Brusa, his friend and fellow workman. The respondent and the deceased, residents of a small town in Connecticut, had come to Barre, Vermont, to work on a road project there in process. One evening, seeking relaxation, they had visited a house in the north end where copious quantities of hard liquor had been consumed, and when they left together to walk the mile or so to reach their rooming house, it was nearly midnight, and both were "feeling no pain." In their somewhat inebriated condition they somehow got to arguing about a watch. As they reached the more thickly settled portion of the city the argument took on real bitterness, and they halted their course to do full justice to the dispute. Shortly, they were in physical combat. In the fracas the respondent stabbed the deceased through the heart with a pocketknife, from which injury the victim later died.

Pironi, becoming frightened after realizing the seriousness of Brusa's injury, foolishly fled from the scene, buried the knife in a garden outside his rooming house, and, later when questioned by the police, denied any knowledge of the affair. When finally confronted with inescapable evidence of his presence at or near the scene of the fracas, he broke down and told the story of the affair in detail.

He claimed that during the combat Brusa had succeeded in getting Pironi down on his back on the sidewalk and that Brusa had one hand around Pironi's throat, the other hand holding one of Pironi's arms, and was trying to crush Pironi's chest by bringing his knee down on Pironi's chest with great force. While in this position, Pironi claimed that with his free hand he had extracted his knife from his pocket, opened it, and struck at Brusa's chest just as Brusa's body came down with great force in his attempt to crush Pironi's chest with his knee. If this story was true, it was a reasonable case of self-defense. But, there being no corroboration, the story had to be told with a ring of truth, and the jury would naturally test every word and gesture of the respondent to determine its truth or falsity.

During the various interviews that we had with Pironi in the preparation of the case, he somehow got the idea that we doubted his ability to get the knife out of his pocket and to open it with one hand as he had claimed. To prove to us that he could do exactly as he claimed, he insisted upon reenacting the drama. We had no doubt of his ability after watching his exhibition. Pironi was so pleased at being able to convince us that he requested to be allowed to perform the same exhibition before the jury. We refused. The reason for our refusal was that the knife was a particularly lethal-looking weapon for one to use only as a pocketknife, and Pironi showed altogether too much skill in its use to please us. We feared that the jury might draw some unfortunate inferences as to the warlike propensities of our client, and so we steadfastly refused to agree that he should perform the exhibition in front of the jury. Pironi was much annoyed at us for our refusal.

Carver, then attorney general, was one of the prosecuting attorneys. During his cross-examination of Pironi, Carver handed the opened knife to Pironi and asked him to "tell the jury just how you held the knife when you struck Brusa." Carver's purpose was twofold: to get the weapon into the hand of the respondent in the hope that it would upset him emotionally, and also possibly to show by his exhibition of the position in which the knife was held some inconsistency with other parts of his story. Pironi eagerly grasped the knife, and, from the expression of his face, it was apparent that he was going to seize the opportunity to put one over on his counsel and enact the demonstration of his ability to open the knife with one hand, which we had denied him. Pretending to misunderstand Carver's question, Pironi closed the knife, put it in his right pocket, descended from the witness chair, and lay down on his back on the floor directly in front of the jury box, jabbering in mixed Italian and English a rapid description of his movements. Every eye in the courtroom was on him. Rapidly and quite effectively he reenacted each movement preceding the moment of the fatal blow.

As he approached the point when he was to extract the knife from his pocket and open it with one hand, Gleason and I held our breaths. Silently we formed a joint prayer that the demonstration would not be performed with too much dexterity. Our prayers were answered—too well. He extracted the knife from his pocket, but, whether from nervousness or as the result of our prayers or for what reason I know not, try as hard as he could, he just couldn't open the blade at all. Beads of sweat appeared on his forehead, and slowly his expression changed from confidence to fear and despair. The moment was heavy with drama as every person in the courtroom watched him intently. Suddenly, realizing the position in which his failure before the jury had put him he lost control of himself, began to babble hysterically, and then to cry like a child. He let out a wild shriek and lapsed into unconsciousness.

As the court hurriedly called a recess and ordered the sheriff to summon medical attention, Gleason and I mentally cursed the perverse impulse that had caused Pironi to violate our instructions. We were quite sure that the exhibition would destroy all confidence of the jury in his story and in him and would likely result in a verdict of first-degree murder.

After long consultation with Pironi's family and friends, we advised that Pironi authorize us to negotiate with the prosecuting officers to see if by a plea of guilty to manslaughter we might yet prevent a first-degree verdict. Reluctantly Pironi gave his consent, and we secured an agreement that the state would recommend a sentence of only two years if he would enter a plea of guilty to manslaughter. The court approved the arrangement, and, the following morning Pironi, fully recovered, pleaded guilty and received a sentence of two years in state's prison.

A few days after the trial Gleason met one of the jury members on the street. The subject of the trial came up for discussion.

"By the way," said the juror, "why did you attorneys let that man plead guilty?"

"Well, we were convinced that his exhibition had prejudiced the jury against him, and we just didn't dare to take the chance of a first-degree conviction."

"Why, you got us all wrong," said the juror. "Every man on the jury felt sorry for him and if we had voted then there would have been a unanimous vote of not guilty."

And we thought that we had understood jury psychology!

Clients Sometimes Tell the Truth

It is widely believed that much that is testified to from the witness chair is false. I have seen and heard my full share of false testimony and occasionally, as trial counsel, have been the unfortunate victim of its sordid practice, and on those occasions it was perhaps natural to experience for short periods a rather sickening disillusionment with the human race. And yet, upon reflection I am confirmed in the opinion that outright falsehood in court is on the whole less common than is generally thought. I do not mean that "the whole truth and nothing but the truth" is common. Far from it. Probably in the great majority of cases that are sharply contested on the facts there is a disrespectable quantity of half-truths, shadings, exaggeration, and coloring that all add up to something far different from the "unvarnished truth." But, after all, this is nothing different from what prevails universally outside of the courtroom in the daily affairs of people.

People remain human beings even when they sit in the witness chair, in spite of the solemn oath they take or of the threatened pains and penalties of perjury. But making up a story out of whole cloth with a deliberate and malicious intent to commit perjury is rather rare in the courtroom. Moreover, it is a great compliment to our system of administering justice that such a large proportion of those fabrications are in one way or another exposed. Sometimes the exposé is the result of brilliance displayed by opposing counsel; sometimes it is the result of accident; more often it is the result of penetrating insight on the part of jury members; and sometimes it is the natural result of a system which, with all its defects, is nevertheless the best that humans have been able to devise and one which has been slowly and gradually evolved through the ages out of the experience of generations. The incident that follows illustrates how the deliberate and "whole cloth" liar is sometimes exposed by the unpredictable vagaries of chance.

Shortly after being admitted to the bar and while still in that fullness of inexperience, confusion, doubt, and incompetence that is the unhappy lot of every beginner at the law, I was employed by a young farmer to bring a suit to collect the sum of $200 alleged to be due for a quantity of logs that had been sold for telephone poles. Brown, my client, had delivered the poles, pursuant to agreement, at the mill of the defendant, Hutchins, in the Town of Wolcott. Upon completion of delivery he had called to collect the purchase price and was then told that the poles did not meet the specifications laid down in the agreement. Hutchins claimed that the agreement was that the poles should be not less than twenty-five feet in length and not less than eight inches in diameter at the small, or top, end. Brown was surprised and shocked at this because he claimed that the agreement was that the poles were to be not less than six inches in diameter at the top, or small, end.

In the course of my first interview with Brown I learned that the agreement had been verbally made and that the whole discussion had taken place at Brown's farm and in the presence of Draper, a hired man who worked for Brown. Both Brown and Draper insisted that no other witnesses had been present, and, in my youth and inexperience, I assumed that the corroboration of Draper's testimony would balance the scales easily in favor of Brown.

The suit was brought before a justice of the peace, and, under the statute, the trial necessarily had to be held in the Town of Wolcott because both parties resided there. A jury was demanded by both parties, which under Vermont practice consisted of six persons instead of twelve as is customary in courts of general jurisdiction. The place of trial was fixed by the justice to be at the Town Hall. On the designated day the parties, counsel, and witnesses repaired to the Town Hall. It was a bitter cold day in January. A fire had been built in the ancient furnace that comprised the only heating facilities, but, because of age, disuse, and other mechanical defects, the furnace was wholly inadequate to cope with the thirty below zero weather that confronted us, and it became quickly apparent that the Town Hall could not be used except at the risk of pneumonia.

Wolcott village, consisting of only a few small stores and buildings, had no other suitable public place to accommodate this important event. The justice was reminded that there was a large waiting room in the railroad station that was well heated by a big, old-fashioned iron stove. Such a place seemed, in the enlightened view of the justice, to satisfy our physical needs and also to be sufficiently public in character as to constitute a fitting and proper temple of public justice. Surely we would not be interfered with by passengers because only one train each day passed through Wolcott.

In short order, chairs and tables being supplied from the general store, the waiting room was readied for its unique service, and all hands moved there for the show. A justice trial has always possessed strong attractions and high entertainment value for those who live in rural villages. There was a day when justice trials and church activities furnished the major part of the social and community life of the Vermont countryside.

The jury having been selected by the customary haphazard and democratic process of having the constable pick likely individuals within the call of his voice, and being properly and solemnly sworn to do their duty, the trial got under way.

After a short opening statement to the jury I put Brown and his hired man on the stand to tell their version of the talk on which the agreement was based. They told their stories simply and effectively and were not in the least disturbed by the cross-examination of Nelson, the defendant's attorney. Upon the conclusion of the testimony of these two witnesses we rested our case, and Nelson called the defendant to the stand.

It was immediately apparent that the sole issue in the case was the terms of the oral agreement. Hutchins testified flatly that the agreement was to the effect that all poles were to be twenty-five feet long and eight inches in diameter at the small end.

While Hutchins was giving his testimony the attention of the courtroom was diverted by the merry jingle of sleigh bells, and, looking out of the window, I saw a bright red sleigh approaching, pulled by a beautiful pair of chestnut horses at a spanking trot. Seated in the sleigh were two men, one the driver and the other a distinguished-looking gentleman. The latter stepped out, entered the waiting room, and leisurely took a seat. Although he was completely unknown to me, he was apparently well known to the jury members and to most of the people in the room. Moreover, it was apparent that he was regarded by all as a man of standing and influence in the community. Supposing that he was merely an interested spectator, I paid little attention to him until in the closing part of Hutchins's testimony Nelson asked a question that surprised and disturbed me.

"Was there anyone else present during this talk besides you, Brown, and Draper?"

"Yes, sir," said Hutchins.

"Who was it?"

"Mr. John Foster."

As the eyes of the jurors automatically turned toward the distinguished-looking gentleman who had recently entered, it was painfully apparent that he was Foster. As I later learned Foster was a lumber and real estate dealer who, by force of an acquisitive talent and much intelligence and cunning, had amassed a sizable amount of this world's goods and was a power to be reckoned with in the political and business life of this rural country.

Immediately upon the conclusion of Hutchins's testimony Foster was called to the stand and sworn. With much poise and with complete assurance he testified that he was present on the occasion of the conversation in question and proceeded to corroborate in detail Hutchins's version of the same.

I was much annoyed at my client. He had told me that no one was present except himself, Hutchins, and the hired man. I am sure that my annoyance was plainly visible as I leaned over to whisper to Brown.

"Why didn't you tell me about this?"

"I never saw this man before in my life," said Brown.

I thought that Brown was lying to me, and the wisdom of the old adage "Don't try to fool your own lawyer" was never more impressed on me than during those uncomfortable minutes while Foster was finishing his direct testimony. I felt that the case was lost, and there was little comfort in knowing that it was the fault of the client and not mine. A trial lawyer always identifies completely with his or her cause and, to a large extent, with the client. I have a strong conviction that most lawyers feel their defeats far more keenly than do the clients who suffer the actual monetary or other punitive penalties.

And yet, as I thought the matter over, it seemed inconceivable that Brown should intentionally deceive me in such circumstances. And so, I suddenly decided to take a long chance on the assumption that perhaps—just perhaps—Brown was telling the truth. As I grew older I learned that it is a pretty good rule of action for a lawyer to have faith in his own client. He will be rewarded thereby more often than not, particularly when the circumstances are such that dishonesty would be stupid.

Brown, though a farmer, did not look the part. His dress, his manner, his speech, and his countenance bore the appearance to be expected of an indoor occupation. He looked more like a bookkeeper than a farmer. Actually, he had not been farming long. He was a college graduate who had developed a yen for farming and had taken a course in agriculture after completing his liberal arts education and had only recently come to Wolcott. He had not lived the rugged life long enough to take on the unmistakable stamp of his occupation. Draper, on the other hand, looked and acted like a farmer. His clothes, his bronze face, his cast of countenance, and even the way he sat proclaimed him to be a farmer.

Brown sat next to me at the table, and just beyond sat Draper. Whispering to Brown, I directed him to quietly and inconspicuously leave his place and go around the ticket office into the adjoining room and stay there. As soon as he left

I began to whisper to Draper, attempting to act as much like an attorney conferring with his client as possible. At the conclusion of Foster's direct testimony I rose to cross-examine. Slowly and with infinite detail, I made him tell again all of his original story. In doing so, of course, I violated one of the cardinal rules of good advocacy. I was sure that everybody in the room was feeling sorry for me. When this boring and deadly recital was finally ended, I paused for several minutes in an attempt to recapture the jury's attention.

"Mr. Foster, you were present on this occasion long enough to get a pretty good look at Mr. Brown, were you not?"

"I think so."

"You could identify Mr. Brown anywhere, could you not?"

"Oh, yes."

"Have you seen Mr. Brown here today?"

"Yes, sir, " he smilingly answered.

"Will you please point him out?"

Without the slightest hesitation he pointed straight at Draper, the hired man!

Justice Is Not Logic

Justice Oliver Wendell Holmes once wrote: "The life of the law is not logic, it is experience." Lawyers who have tried jury cases would agree. Logic is an aid to the determination of what is justice, but jurors seldom make the mistake of becoming so preoccupied with logic as to miss the larger question of what is broad justice. They are much more at home in the field of experience than they are in the field of logic.

One morning in the days of my early practice I received a telephone call from Abner Downs, a farmer who lived in Washington some eight miles from Barre. It was an SOS call. Downs informed me that he had been arrested on a criminal warrant, charging breach of the peace and criminal assault and was, at the very time of his call, in the toils of the law. The warrant had been issued by the state's attorney of Orange County, returnable before John Frazer, Esq., justice of the peace, and, having been hailed into court, he was informed that the court proposed to try him immediately. Abner implored me to come to Washington posthaste and rescue him from the calamity that threatened. Disaster seemed so imminent from Abner's tone of voice that there appeared to be no time to learn the facts over the telephone, so I drove to Washington village immediately to learn what it was all about.

The justice of the peace insisted that I should proceed with the drawing of the jury before I was even to have a chance to discuss the case with my client. While the constable was out rounding up the jurors who had been called, I hurriedly conferred with Abner in an attempt to find out what the facts were. Actually, I had discovered upon arriving in Washington that I had two clients instead of one, for Abner's son, William, had also been arrested and charged as a joint respondent in the commission of what was described in the complaint as a most deadly assault.

From Abner's account it appeared that bad blood had existed between Abner and one William Renfrew, a blacksmith who plied his trade in a small blacksmith shop just on the edge of the village of Washington. On the day charged in the complaint Abner and his son William had driven to Washington village to carry their milk to the creamery. As they left the village and started up the hill road home they came by Renfrew's shop. Renfrew, who was working in his yard heating an iron rim for a wagon wheel, noticed Abner and William and proceeded to use abusive language. Abner and William believed more in deeds than in words. Pulling the old gray mare to a halt, Abner jumped out of the wagon and started for Renfrew. Renfrew held his ground, and in a twinkling a real battle of fisticuffs was in progress. William, believing that he owed some filial duty in the circumstances, followed his father into the yard with the apparent intention of giving aid and comfort, if it should be needed. The evidence was somewhat conflicting as to the extent to which this aid and comfort was actually furnished by William, but surely there was no conflict in the evidence as to the fact that

Renfrew received a thorough beating in the process, with injuries that laid him up for a couple of weeks. It was useless, of course, to explain to Abner that words, however abusive, are not a defense to physical force. I am sure that he would have been unimpressed.

The first witness for the state was Miss Abigail Fuller, who lived across the street from the blacksmith shop and who, according to her testimony, had observed the entire fracas from the time Renfrew started using his abusive language. She told the story of the combat and of the events leading up to it with an emphasis and with an eye for detail that was truly magnificent. Or, rather, I would have felt so had I not then been acting in the unfortunate position of counsel for the respondent, with a duty to find some mitigating circumstance in his conduct. When her story was finished, it was only too apparent that my task was hopeless.

Then followed the testimony of the victim, Renfrew. All I could do on cross-examination with him was to draw some grudging admissions that perhaps he had used a few insulting words just previous to the fistic combat. At this point the court recessed for lunch.

I called my clients together for a brief conference in which several of their staunchest supporters participated. There never was any question in our minds but that, no matter how much the law might condemn the conduct of my clients, truly in the larger sense there was every justification for what had been done. Sadly enough there was hardly a thing in the whole testimony of the star witness and the complainant with which either of my clients disagreed in basis of fact. In that situation there would seem to be little use in putting them on the stand. And yet, as a practical situation, I had to put up some show of defense. Finally in desperation I said to one of Abner's close friends, a storekeeper, "What kind of a reputation does this man Renfrew have here in town?"

"He's the biggest liar in Orange County," said Jones, the storekeeper.

"Would you be willing to testify to that?"

"I certainly would. I'd be glad to."

"Well," I said, "do you suppose you could line up a few witnesses here during the noon hour who would be willing to take the stand and testify as to his reputation for truthfulness?"

"How many do you want?" said Jones.

"Oh, I would like to have at least three or four, if possible."

"I'll have 'em here," said Jones, "by the time court is ready to convene."

When we returned from lunch I found that Jones had made good on his promise with a generosity that was truly admirable. He had eighteen men, all citizens of the town, who were all ready, willing, and anxious to take the stand and tell the jury (they probably already knew it) about the bad reputation that Renfrew had for honesty. One by one these witnesses were put on the stand and asked concerning Renfrew's honesty.

"Does Mr. Renfrew have a reputation in this vicinity for truth and honesty?" The answer was invariably, "Yes, sir."

"What is his reputation?"

"He's the biggest liar in Orange County."

At the conclusion of the testimony of the eighteen witnesses, who had testified to nothing except Renfrew's truth and veracity, I rested the case without putting either of the respondents on the stand or any other witnesses to testify or to dispute in any way what had been already testified to by the state's witness. After a short charge from the justice of the peace, in which he practically told the jury to find a verdict of guilty, the jury retired. They were out exactly ten minutes and then filed back into the courtroom ready to report.

"Have you agreed upon a verdict?" said the justice to the foreman.

"We have, your Honor."

"What is your verdict?"

"Not guilty," said the foreman.

What Is Memory?

Memory is a tricky thing. Psychologists know this. So do trial lawyers. A large part of forensic success consists of probing the accuracy of memory. More often than not this probing is not to establish that a witness is lying. It is to uncover the weaknesses of memory of an honest person.

Clarence Bixby of Moretown came in to consult his favorite lawyer, William Lord, Esq., of Montpelier. He said that he had sold a pair of horses to Jeremiah Jones and had taken back a chattel mortgage for $300 which had represented part of the purchase price. After a year or so Jones had concluded that his farming venture had been a failure, and so he had decided to sell his farm, stock, tools, and machinery at public auction, which he had proceeded to do. At that time $250 had still been due and unpaid on the mortgage. The pair of horses had been sold along with all the other property, but nothing had been paid to Bixby from the proceeds to cover the balance due on the mortgage. The horses had been bid off at auction by a horse dealer from Warren named Smith, who had in turn sold the horses at private sale.

After considerable time had elapsed and no payment was forthcoming, Bixby consulted his lawyer to ascertain his legal rights. His lawyer explained that Bixby had a choice of three possible remedies. One was to bring suit against Jones, another was to bring an action in replevin against the present possessor of the horses to repossess the horses, and a third alternative was to bring suit against Smith in an action for "conversion" of the horses to recover their value. Bixby quickly recognized that his best choice would be to sue Smith, because Smith was a man of property and "good" for the amount in question, and he didn't want the horses back in any case if he could avoid it. He so informed Lord, who then went on to explain that there was one condition precedent to his right to recover from Smith.

"You see, Mr. Bixby, unless Smith knew of the mortgage he would be an innocent purchaser for value. And if he was an innocent purchaser for value you could not recover unless you protested the selling of the horses at the time they were put up to bid. If you were there and let the horses be sold, the law would presume that this was a waiver of your rights against Smith."

"Well, Mr. Lord, you just leave it to me. You bring suit against Smith, and when the trial comes I will have a witness that I protested the sale."

In those days Bixby used to be an ardent billiard player and used to frequent Pete's Pool and Billiard Hall, as did a number of his friends. Two of those friends were Joe Swift and Clarence Allen, a couple of retired farmers who used to while away their retirement days in the pool hall. Bixby recalled that both Swift and Allen had been present at the time of the auction. Bixby began to frequent the hall even more than in the past. Whenever Swift or Allen was there he would regale the customers in the hall with the details of his lawsuit, including a vivid description of his stepping up to the auctioneer's stand when the horses were put up for bid and his exact words protesting the sale because of the unpaid mortgage. In the months intervening prior to the trial Bixby took occasion to repeat these words of protest whenever Swift or Allen was present. Usually in such instances he would not appear to be talking to them but to some new willing listener—but always in their presence.

All of this was a complete fabrication. There had been no protest. Bixby did not know at the time that the law required it. Moreover, at no time prior to the trial had Bixby asked Swift and Allen to testify for him, nor had he even asked them if they remembered the protest to the auctioneer. On the day of the trial, after being subpoenaed, Swift and Allen were called to the stand. As each took the stand he was asked by Counselor Lord about the circumstances of the sale and the protest.

"Yes sir, Mr. Lord, Mr. Bixby stepped right up to the auctioneer's stand and said he wanted to say something. The auctioneer said he could. And then Bixby said, 'I protest the sale of this pair of horses because I have an unpaid mortgage on them for $250.'"

Swift and Allen were testifying with complete honesty. Their "memory" of what happened was clear and explicit—even though it never happened in fact. Thus was demonstrated the fragility of that memory which we so easily take for granted. One of its frequent and most dangerous components is the subtle but powerful influence exercised by constant repetition of a plausible untruth.

Don't Fence Me In

Fayette Cutler and his wife, Anne, lived on Central Street in Barre. A portion of the lot on which their home stood cornered on Main and Central streets and was a natural and preferred location for a filling station. One of the major oil companies made the couple a generous offer for the lot, and the Cutlers accepted it. The offer was subject to a search of title and an abstract showing good title.

Cutler came to me to get me to search the title and make an abstract. Actually, the title was clear with one slight exception. The property had come to Mrs. Cutler through the will of her father. The will provided that the property should vest outright in Mrs. Cutler, but that in case Mrs. Cutler should have children the children would take a half interest.

Cutler was 75 years of age and his wife was 73 at the time the title was being searched, and they had never had any children. However, in the eyes of the law birth of a child could not be conclusively negated. With some apprehension I sent the abstract of title along to the oil company, wondering how they would react to the technical defect. In due course Cutler received a letter from the oil company's counsel

reading as follows:

Dear Mr. Cutler:
We have received the abstract of title concerning your land at the corner of North Main and Central streets in Barre, Vermont, which is subject to option by this company.
We note the technical defect in title due to the possibility of children being born to Mrs. Cutler. However, we have noted the special circumstances and have decided that, if you will furnish us an affidavit setting forth these special circumstances in detail, we believe we will be able to waive the defect.

Upon receipt of the letter Cutler sat down and wrote a handwritten letter of reply but decided to bring it up and show it to me before sending it. This is what he wrote:

Dear Mr. ———:
Your letter received. Regarding the special circumstances you mention. I am 75 years of age and my wife is 73. We have been married for 51 years. We have never had any children and we don't expect to. So, if you need an affidavit please make it out and Mrs. Cutler and I will sign it.
                              Very truly yours,
                              (signed) Fayette Cutler
p.s. Please don't put anything in the affidavit to prevent us from trying.

A Fair Trade

Late on a Saturday night in early April a telephone call came
to my home from the Washington County Jail. The plaintive
voice on the other end was that of a young woman who had
been arrested, locked up in jail, and charged with adultery. In
those days adultery was frowned upon by the authorities. The
crime statistics today show very few arrests for that crime.
The woman on the phone begged me to come and see her, as
she needed a lawyer, she said. I calmed her down as best I
could and promised to call on her at the jail Monday.

When I met my client I found her to be a spirited young
woman twenty-four years of age and quite attractive. She
told me the following story. She and her husband and
another married couple had been living in adjoining cabins in
the back mountains of Fayston, where the two husbands had
been employed by a lumber company, cutting and skidding
logs for transportation to the sawmill in the spring. They had
been living there all winter since the job had commenced in
early December. Apparently the isolation had been pretty
complete because of the heavy snow and the impassable
roads. Life had been quite boring. In early March the two

husbands had entered into a bargain to swap wives, and since then the two wives without protest had exchanged cabins and husbands and had appeared to live happily until the authorities had intervened. My client was Mollie and her legal husband was Harry. The other woman was Jane and her legal husband was George.

I asked Mollie how the authorities came to intervene. She explained that in early April Jane had walked to town and complained to the sheriff, who had arrested all four. The other three—Jane, George and Harry—had promptly pleaded guilty to the crime of adultery. The two men were sentenced to Windsor State Prison and Jane to the Women's Reformatory at Rutland. Mollie, for some reason not readily apparent, had pleaded not guilty.

In spite of persistent questioning, I could not find out from Mollie why Jane had ultimately made the complaint after consenting to the arrangement for several weeks. The reluctance of Mollie to give me the answer was puzzling.

It was obvious—if the story was true, and there seemed no reason to doubt it—that all four were guilty. I patiently explained this to Mollie and advised her to plead guilty. But she persisted in her refusal and said that she was entitled to a jury trial. And, of course, she was. So, with some annoyance, I prepared to go through the motions of a defense for her, which I was sure would be an exercise in futility. I was hopeful, with a little time, that she would come to her senses and plead guilty and thus save the state the expense of a trial and save me from the waste of time that would be involved. The trial was scheduled for about three weeks from the time I first interviewed her.

As the trial date drew closer I had another long interview with my client to prepare for the actual trial. Mollie still persisted. She was bound to have a trial. Again I tried to extract from her the reason why Jane had made the complaint. By this time my curiosity had reached fever pitch. As I questioned her further it suddenly dawned on me that there was actually no evidence against Mollie except from the other three participants. The state's attorney was obviously going to have to rely on them to prove the fact of adultery. I wondered. Would the other three wish to testify against Mollie? Under the Constitution no person is compelled to give testimony the effect of which would be to incriminate the individual. But, the other three had already been convicted and were serving time in prison. So how could testimony harm them?

The case was "getting under my skin," and I spent a long evening with the law books and satisfied myself that the three participants could successfully claim their Constitutional privilege and refuse to testify, *if they so desired.* But here was the rub. Would they desire to? And how could I find out? I felt reasonably sure that the two men bore no ill will against Mollie. But I wasn't sure about Jane. After all, she had made the complaint. Moreover, would the other three like to see Mollie get off scot-free when they were paying the penalty? I felt that it would be unethical for me to go to the three other participants and put the idea into their heads, even if they would want to claim privilege and refuse to testify against Mollie. So I asked Mollie how she thought the other three felt about her now.

She told me that Jane had cooled off and was now sorry that she had made the complaint, and she was sure that Jane bore her no ill will.

"How do you know this?" I asked her.

"Because she and Harry and George are right here in the jail with me. The state's attorney had them brought up here for the trial, and I have talked with them several times. Jane don't want to hurt me."

"How about Harry and George?" I asked.

"They feel the same way," she said.

"All right," I said, "you talk again with all three of them. Ask them directly if they want to testify against you. If they say they do not, then you tell them to ask their own lawyer whether they have to testify or not."

Apparently, Mollie knew what she was talking about because the next day Webster Miller, Esq., a very competent lawyer practicing in Montpelier who had represented all three of the other participants at the time they were sentenced, called on the phone. He said that he had interviewed his three clients at their request and that they did not wish to testify against Mollie. He had explained to them the law of Constitutional privilege.

The case came on for trial the next day. The state's attorney began his case by introducing necessary records of marriage and a few routine other things and then immediately called Jane to the stand. After giving her name and a few unimportant details, Jane turned to the judge and said, "I don't want to testify."

"Why not?" inquired the judge.

"Because my testimony would hurt me. It would incriminate me."

At this point Attorney Miller, who was present in court throughout, rose to his feet and informed the court that he was representing Jane and wished to be heard on the question of Constitutional privilege.

After some discussion in open court the judge adjourned the court into his chambers, where a long legal discussion took place between Miller, the state's attorney, and the presiding judge. Finally, the judge ruled that because the complaint to which Jane had pleaded guilty alleged an act of adultery on only one specific date, any testimony given by Jane would have a tendency to incriminate her if prosecution were later brought against Jane for any other acts of adultery on other dates. After all, she had been living together with Harry for several weeks prior to the complaint. So Jane was excused from the stand. In quick succession Harry and then George were called to the stand, the same objection made, and the same ruling made by the judge.

So the state's attorney was left at this point without any more witnesses and without any more evidence. He asked for a continuance to the next morning, which was granted, and the court adjourned for the day.

The next morning when court convened the state's attorney addressed the court and said that he could find no further witnesses or evidence to present and moved to discontinue the case. I objected and filed a motion of my own. The motion was for a directed verdict, which when carried to judgment would bar any future prosecution. My motion was granted, and Mollie was released.

Later, she came to me to thank me for what I had done for her. She had no money, so I thought that an adequate fee would be for her now to tell me why Jane had made the complaint after living with the arrangement for weeks. She agreed.

"Well, you see, Mr. Davis, Jane found out that George had to give Harry a pig to boot. She got pretty mad!"

Undeserved Credit

My appointment as a Superior Court judge was in 1931. The appointment was to fill a vacancy resulting from the elevation of Superior Court Judge Warner Graham to the Supreme Court. I felt that it was a great honor to be given the chance to try to fill the shoes of Judge Graham, for was he not only an excellent practicing lawyer but he became a truly outstanding judge. In addition to great skill as a student, he possessed judicial temperament to a rare degree. He truly earned the unanimous respect he was accorded.

Judge Graham's appointment, and hence mine, came in the middle of the fall term of Windham County Court. I was immediately assigned to preside for the remainder of that term of court, which was being held at the county seat in Newfane. It was a particularly protracted term with a heavy docket of important cases. For this reason the term was necessarily continued past the scheduled date of the opening of Lamoille County Court in Hyde Park, and so the opening date of Lamoille County Court was necessarily deferred a few days beyond the statutory opening date. I was assigned to Lamoille County as well.

It happened, too, that the same court reporter, Mary Cerasoli Storey, was also assigned both to Windham and Lamoille, and so the morning after the business of Windham was concluded Mary and I drove posthaste to Hyde Park to open the fall term there. In the pressure of business I had failed to recall that I would need to make a general charge to the jury when I arrived at Hyde Park. Tradition and practice in those days provided that the presiding judge should make a charge to the whole panel of jurors called for service during the term. The purpose of the charge was to inform the jury members in detail the rules of law and practice that would govern them in the discharge of their duties during the term. Because the Windham term was in process when I was appointed, I had not yet had the experience of making such a charge. So I was not really prepared to face the task in Lamoille.

Faced with this frightening prospect, Mary Storey promptly came to my rescue. She pointed out that she had taken stenographic notes of the last general charge made in Lamoille by the judge previously presiding and that immediately upon arriving at Hyde Park, while I was attending to other details associated with the opening of court, she would transcribe those notes in time for me to use in making the required charge.

What a relief! True to her word, Mary produced an accurate and verbatim transcript of that charge in ample time and handed it to me. Because I was a new judge and rather young as well, I read the charge with great emphasis and oratorical profundity. In fact, I even impressed myself.

The county clerk, a gracious lady of long service, had of course heard this charge delivered the term before by Judge John C. Sherburne, who wrote it. On completion of the charge the court took a brief recess, during which the associate judges, the county clerk, and one or two others gathered in the room assigned as the judge's chambers. The county clerk with obvious sincerity said, "Judge, I want to congratulate you on that charge to the jury. I have been here many years and have heard many good charges, but that is the best one I ever heard."

I hope that the reader will forgive me for not explaining to her that the charge I gave was word for word the exact language she had heard delivered the term before by Judge Sherburne.

Where His Duty Was

One of the stories that used to circulate around the courthouse about Judge Harland B. Howe has to do with the problems of a farmer jury member who was called for jury duty and needed to be excused. I cannot vouch for the truth of the story, but it circulated so widely and for so long and was so consistent with the personality of the judge that I have recorded it here.

One morning, a half hour or so before court was to convene, Allen Martin, U.S. district attorney, noticed a man nervously walking about the hall of the courthouse. His so-apparent nervousness prompted Martin to accost the gentleman and see if he could be of any assistance to him. The man turned out to be a farmer from Jericho who had been called to serve at the then-current term of court. The farmer told Martin that it was impossible for him to serve and that he didn't know what to do.

"Why can't you serve?" Martin inquired.

"Well, you see I have a farm with thirty-five milking cows and no hired man. My wife would usually do the milking and the chores while I would be away, but she's going to have a baby any day now, and besides, in her condition, it wouldn't be safe for her to be doing any heavy work.''

"You come with me," said Martin. "I'll take you in to see the judge. He's the only man who can excuse you."

Whereupon Martin ushered the juror into the judge's chambers, introduced him to the judge, and explained that the man wanted to be excused from jury service.

"Why can't you serve?" asked the judge.

The juror was very much agitated at being in such unfamiliar surroundings and in the presence of the distinguished-looking judge, and in his nervousness and confusion he blurted out, "Well you see, Your Honor, my wife is about to become pregnant.''

"What?" roared the judge.

Martin came to his rescue. "He means, Your Honor, that his wife is about to become confined."

"Oh," said the judge. "Well, anyway, in either case he ought to be to home. So he's excused."

A Little Question of Sanity

Vermont, like many of her sister states, inherited much of her divorce law from England. Among those principles inherited which are still in force is the principle of condonation. Reduced to its simplest terms, the principle of condonation is that when one party to the marriage contract has been guilty of an offense against the marriage relation, if the other party "cohabits" with the offending party knowing that the offense has been committed, such conduct amounts to a forgiveness or, as the law defines it, condonation. Once the offense has been condoned, the parties start all over again "from scratch."

Another rule that was in effect in Vermont until changed by statute was that when either party to the marriage was insane a divorce could not be obtained. This latter rule was changed by statute since the time of the following episode.

Mrs. Jessie Whalen brought her petition to the Woodstock County Court praying for divorce against her husband, John, alleging that John had been guilty of intolerable severity. The case came on to be heard before the County Court. Judge Allen R. Sturtevant, then a Superior

Court judge, later an associate justice of the Supreme Court, presided. The case was uncontested.

The plaintiff's counsel was a well-known lawyer whom I will call Fred Sanborn. Sanborn was fortunate in his client. She was a remarkably good-looking woman, beautiful of face and beautiful of figure. Following the customary procedure, the petitioner took the stand first and, under questioning by her counsel, portrayed a series of brutal acts committed by her husband. It was an unusually strong case. Seemingly, it was bulletproof. Sanborn became so carried away with the dramatic story that his client was telling and with the impression that she was obviously creating that he committed one fatal mistake, He asked one question too many.

"Have you seen your husband lately?" said Sanborn. It was obvious that he expected his client to answer in the negative. It was equally obvious that it was something of a surprise to him when she answered, "Yes." Recognizing immediately that further inquiry along this line had better be abandoned, Sanborn walked nonchalantly to his seat at the petitioner's table and sat down.

Although Judge Sturtevant was the kind of a judge who never seems to be listening to a witness, those who have practiced before him will tell you that very little escapes his ears. He has a strongly developed sensitiveness to the implications in situations disclosed by testimony and a well-developed imagination. The petitioner's answer to the last question did not escape him. Turning slowly toward the witness, he obviously intended to follow through the suggestion contained in the last answer:

"When was it, Mrs. Whalen, that you last saw your husband?"

"About two months ago," she replied.

"Tell us something about the circumstances, how you

116

happened to see him then."

"Well, you see," she said, "I was staying with my sister in Northfield, and my husband drove up one day and told me he was going to Burlington on business and asked me if I would like to ride up to Burlington with him to see my brother."

"Did you go?"

"Oh, yes, Your Honor."

"How long did you stay?"

"Oh, just overnight."

"Did your husband stay, too?"

"Yes."

"Where did you stay overnight?"

"I stayed with my brother in Burlington."

"Where did your husband stay?"

"Oh, he stayed there, too."

"Did you both occupy the same room?"

"Oh, yes, Your Honor."

"Did you both occupy the same bed?"

"Oh, yes, Your Honor."

At this point there was a distinct pause in the sequence of the questions. The audience looked expectant and Sanborn looked worried. Finally the judge looked up and said, "I guess that disposes of your case, doesn't it, Mr. Sanborn?"

"Just a minute, Your Honor," replied Mr. Sanborn, as he got slowly to his feet and shuffled up to the witness chair. "I would like to speak to the witness privately."

Without waiting for the court's permission Sanborn and the witness started a whispered consultation. Finally a beautiful smile broke out over Sanborn's countenance, and he walked directly up to the bench and addressed Judge Sturtevant in a whisper. "Well, it's all right, your honor," said Sanborn.

"It's all right?" said Judge Sturtevant. "What do you

mean, it's all right?"

"Well, nothing happened," he said.

Judge Sturtevant paused a moment and then slowly shook his head. "No," he said. "We couldn't grant a divorce in a situation like this, Mr. Sanborn."

Sanborn's face fell, and he turned and walked back to his seat at the table. He had a most dejected appearance. There was a long silence as he sat there in a brown study. Suddenly he got up and marched to the bench and again addressed Judge Sturtevant, this time aloud so that all in the courtroom could hear. "But I don't understand, Your Honor."

"You don't understand?" said Judge Sturtevant.

"No," said Sanborn, "I don't understand why you can't grant a divorce in a situation like this."

"Well," said the judge, "you understand if something had happened that we couldn't grant a divorce, don't you?"

"Oh, yes," said Sanborn.

Slowly the judge turned to the client seated in the witness chair, and it was perfectly apparent by his look and gesture that he fully comprehended and appreciated her beautiful face and figure. "Well, if nothing did happen, the man's crazy, and we can't grant a divorce against a crazy man."

Breach of Promise

Hank Osgood was a Vermont individualist of the old school. He operated a farm outside St. Johnsbury. He was quite successful, took good care of his money, and gradually got together quite a sizable bank account, a fact that was well known to his friends and neighbors. At the time of the bank holiday in the 1930s several of his friends came over to commiserate with him at the great loss that they expected he would experience as a result of having his large bank account tied up. Hank was quite unperturbed, and this lack of concern puzzled his friends because they knew how well Hank loved money. Several months later they learned why. Hank had had some kind of a premonition of coming trouble in the country and had drawn out all his money and buried it under an apple tree in his yard.

Hank was single, never having been married. He had an excellent housekeeper, who had been with him for a long time and who, incidentally, was also single. Eventually the neighbors noticed that Sadie was no longer around. And soon the rumor reached the neighborhood that Sadie had brought suit against Hank for breach of promise of marriage.

The rumor turned out to be true.

In due course the case came up for trial by jury in Caledonia County Court. In order to bolster the claim for damages it was alleged that Hank and Sadie had had sexual relations. When Hank was put on the stand to testify in his own defense, his counsel asked him if it was true that he and Sadie had engaged in sexual relations. He admitted that it was true.

"Well, tell us, Hank, in your own words just how did this happen?"

"All right. You see, Mr. Porter, Sadie was my housekeeper. Good housekeeper she were. Good cook, too. Last winter I was lumbering up on the Adams lot. Good and cold it were. One day it were colder'n usual, and I was late gittin home and gittin the chores done. So when I finally got into the house I was cold and tired and hungry. Sadie made me a good supper—a real good supper. After supper I felt sleepy and went right up to bed. I was so tired. After I got to bed Sadie came upstairs and came right into my room. She opened the window a little, smoothed the curtains, straightened out things on the table beside my bed. Then she straightened up my clothes, which I had thrown over the chair, and hung them up in the closet. I kept saying, 'Sadie, I'm tired, I wanna go to sleep. G'wan downstairs and let me sleep.' But she kept stayin'. And then she came over and sat on the edge of my bed and began stroking my forehead. I kept sayin', 'Sadie, I'm tired, go away, I want to go to sleep.' But she kept teasin', and teasin', and teasin'. And finally I guv in."

Justice Powers

In 1936 I resigned from the bench. This decision was one of the hardest of my life. I loved the law and I loved the work as a judge. But my salary as a judge had been reduced from $5,000 to $4,200, as were the salaries of all the judges of the Superior Court. This was part of a general salary reduction made applicable to all state officers and employees in order to balance the state budget. This kind of an approach would be unthinkable today. Superior Court judges are paid $35,550 per annum today. In any event I could see no possible way that I could provide a college education for my two children on that salary.

Before my decision was announced I received a telephone call from Chief Justice George M. Powers of the Supreme Court. He asked me to come to Montpelier for an interview. Apparently, he had picked up a rumor of my impending resignation.

When I arrived at the judge's chambers he asked me very bluntly if I intended to resign. I replied in the affirmative. Thereupon he gave me a long and bristling lecture. I cannot now remember ever being scolded more fiercely or more skillfully by anyone, not even my father, who was an expert in that field. Most of the scolding was directed at pointing out how badly I was letting the state down. When I felt that he had taken off every last shred of skin on my body he suddenly paused.

"Is your decision final?" he asked.

"Yes."

"Then I just want to say if I was in your exact place, I'd do the same thing."

A Difficult Assignment

After more than a week of trial a sharply contested case was finally nearing its end. Final arguments of counsel were completed, and court adjourned a bit early in the afternoon. The following morning at nine o'clock the presiding judge would deliver his charge to the jury.

The purpose of a judge's charge under the American system is to declare and define the law applicable to the case and to summarize the principal issues and the evidence bearing on those issues. The judge must faithfully refrain from expressing an opinion on the facts or the issues that are factual in nature, for that is the exclusive function of the jury. The jury, on the other hand, is to accept the law as laid down by the judge and apply it to the facts as they find them.

All of us engaged in the trial were housed in the same hotel. About ten thirty in the evening my telephone rang. It was the presiding judge calling. His voice was a bit thick. He asked me if I would come to his room. Lawyers customarily respond to a request from the presiding judge with alacrity; and I did.

Knocking on the door of his room and being invited to

enter, I found an unusual sight. The judge was stretched at full length on the bed with papers and law books scattered all over the bed in great disorder.

The judge was deep in his cups.

"What can I do for you, Judge?" I asked.

"I want you to write my charge."

You can well imagine that I was considerably startled by this request. For the judge to ask anyone to write his charge for him was unorthodox, but to ask one of the lawyers in the case was shocking. I was extremely uncomfortable. I began to speculate as to how I could possibly extricate myself from this unhappy situation. I certainly did not want to offend the judge by refusing. Neither did I want to have the judge embarrassed if he should arrive in court the next morning with no charge ready to deliver to the jury.

"Judge," I said, "you just rest awhile, and then you'll be able to write the charge yourself."

"Now, you know damn well I'm in no condition to write the charge. Will you or won't you?"

"But, Judge, I'm afraid it would not be entirely proper for me to do that."

"Proper? Well now, I'll be the judge of that. It'll be a lot more proper than if I were to try to write it in my present condition."

"But, Judge, can't you get anybody else to do it? I shouldn't be the one to do it."

"You know I can't get anybody else to do it. It has to be somebody that has been all the way through the case. And you're the only one that has been a judge. You know how to go about it."

My mental turmoil was acute. How could I refuse this request without subjecting the judge to great embarrassment? He was in no condition to write the charge or accept "no" for an answer. After all, in the last analysis it was the judge's responsibility, and I tried to comfort myself by the thought that, after he received the charge from me and was in full possession of his faculties in the morning, he could correct anything I had written that needed to be corrected or possibly find some excuse to recess the court until he could write the charge himself. So, most reluctantly, I agreed to do it.

"Good," he said. "Now you write my charge tonight, and in the morning you meet me in the dining room for breakfast promptly at eight o'clock. Now, you write a good fair charge, mind you," was the judge's parting shot, as I went back to my room and with great trepidation prepared to carry out this bizarre assignment.

How I sweated!

I did my level best to disassociate myself from my status as attorney for the defendant and assume the attitude and posture of an impartial judge. It was not easy. It was two o'clock in the morning before I finally went to bed. As I turned and tossed, unable to sleep, a new fear assailed me. Had I leaned so far over backward trying to be fair that I had perhaps in some way compromised my client's interest? What a night of mental suffering—and not a wink of sleep.

Morning finally came. As I showered and shaved and yawned my sleepless night showed clearly on my countenance as it looked back at me from the bathroom mirror.

I joined the judge in the dining room as he had directed. He invited me to sit down at his table and have breakfast with him, which I did. I quickly looked the judge over, wondering how he came through the night. To my surprise his condition contrasted sharply with mine. He was freshly shaved, clear-eyed, rested, and looking as fresh as a daisy. I wondered then why I had ever resigned from the bench.

"Well," said the judge, "have you got my charge?"

"Here it is," I said, and I handed over the folded sheets of yellow legal paper on which I had worked most of the night. He took it and promptly slipped it into the inside pocket of his suit jacket without even looking at it.

Nervously, I waited for him to complete his breakfast and at least to read the results of my hours of work. But the judge was unconcerned and full of small talk. Finally, about fifteen minutes before nine o'clock he rose and said, "Well, I guess we better get over to court."

I followed him over to the courthouse and watched him enter the judge's chambers about three minutes before nine. I took my place at the counsel table with my heart pounding. Promptly at nine the bell rang, the presiding judge majestically mounted the bench, seated himself comfortably, reached into his coat pocket, pulled out the yellow sheets on which was my charge, and with great articulation read to the jury word for word the charge as I had written it.

My client won—*in spite of the charge.*

Trial Procedure—A Comparison between the American and the English System

Mention has been made before of the Honorable John Garibaldi Sargent of Ludlow, a friend of President Coolidge and attorney general of the United States. I had great respect for Sargent. He was not only a great student of the law but one of the most widely read men I ever knew. He was the soul of honor. And he was one of the most skillful triers at the bar.

For several years prior to his death he was physically disabled, but his disability had nothing to do with his mental powers. He retained them to the end. He practiced law from his bedside for quite a while in Ludlow. I remember once, when I was a Superior Court judge, that he had a chancery case of great importance. To permit him to continue to act as counsel for his client I allowed the case to be tried in his bedroom in Ludlow, which was a large room over his garage. He examined witnesses and argued points of law while reclining in bed. As far as I could see he was exercising all the skill that he had hitherto shown in court under more usual circumstances.

Later, I remember calling on him while he was confined in the Mary Fletcher Hospital in Burlington, now the Medical Center Hospital of Vermont. His room was littered with law books and other reading matter, which showed that he was trying to live a normal life in spite of his disabling illness. We talked about many things, but the thing I remember best was his dissertation on the differences between the English system of advocacy and that pertaining in this country. He said that in one respect he felt the English system to be superior.

This remark surprised me, so I pressed him for more details. He called attention to the fact that in the English system the lawyers are divided into two classes: attorneys and barristers. The attorneys are the ones who make all the contact with the clients, and the barristers are those who actually try cases for clients in the courts. One respect in which he thought the English system superior had a psychological aspect to it. In the American system the lawyer has all the contact with the client, interviews the witnesses, and then, if the case is tried, also appears in court as advocate and actually tries the case. In the English system the barrister never talks with the client or the witnesses until they come into court. He is furnished with carefully prepared written briefs by the attorney.

Sargent pointed out that when the American lawyer questions a witness he has already seen and who has told the story in detail, he often has great difficulty in getting the witness to tell the story anew in court. The reason is that subconsciously the witness is aware of having already told the story to the lawyer and hence is prone to omit many details. Also, the witness never tells the story with quite the same earnestness and conviction because now it is a twice-told story.

In the English system, the witness is now confronted with a new face and personality. And, subconsciously aware that the barrister has not heard the story in person before, the witness tells it with all the vividness and emphasis of a first telling. Because the law does not permit the counsel to cross-examine his own witness, the result is a far more forceful, complete, and vivid portrayal under the English system.

This comment is not intended to say that the English system overall is superior to the American system but merely to point out this one psychological advantage the English system gives to the English lawyer over the American lawyer, who tries the case in court and participates in the preliminary interviews as well.

Delays of the Law Can Be Overcome

Not many people remember what a power the farmers were in the legislature in the old days. That was long before the intensive in-migration that has taken place in Vermont during the last two decades. But in those days, which were the heyday of the family farm, the members of the house were elected one from each town, and the small and medium-sized towns were mostly agricultural, so, naturally, farmers constituted the large majority of the members of the House and represented the life and culture of the times in Vermont. They were good legislators, too, not easily fooled and with a degree of common sense greatly to be admired. But they ran the show, so to speak.

In many cases leadership for their political interests was supplied by the Farm Bureau in the person of Arthur Packard, long-time knowledgeable and canny president of the bureau.

Most of the marketing of milk in Vermont came eventually to be done through farm cooperatives, of which the farmers were members. But a substantial amount of milk was still purchased and shipped and sold through independent milk companies, such as Hood & Company, Whiting Milk Company, and others. And when a particularly difficult time came for the farmers to get a living price for their milk a war broke out between the cooperatives and the independents. In an attempt to further unify the farmers and put them in a better bargaining position, a large group undertook to set up a new and large cooperative, which was to embrace all farmers, and which was called MILK, Inc. To prevent this proposed new and large cooperative from being successful, some of the independent milk companies served notice on the farmers who were selling their milk to the independents that if they joined MILK, Inc., they would not be allowed to sell their milk to the independent company. If successful this rule would greatly limit the effectiveness of MILK, Inc. But in some areas of the state the only creameries were owned by the independents, and if the independent in such an area refused to accept the milk, this refusal would spell disaster for the farmers of the area.

Something was needed to stop these threats if MILK, Inc., was to be organized with all farmers in the state as members. Arthur Packard was then at the very height of his power and leadership in the state. He came to the rescue.

Late at night I received a telephone call from Packard after I had retired. He wanted to come and see me about what he called an emergency. Sleepily and somewhat reluctantly, I invited him to come. He explained the situation to me in his usual perceptive and articulate manner. I happened to have a copy of *Vermont General Laws* at home. I pulled it down and studied the milk statutes already in force. I found one that made it a criminal offense for a milk distributor to give different prices for the same kind of milk to different shippers. By the simple insertion of the words "or who refuses to accept milk from any producer solely because he becomes a member of a cooperative," it would produce a statute that would make it illegal to do what some of the independents were doing and would serve the purpose of the farmers. I pointed this out to Packard, and he was delighted. I remarked that it would be difficult to get the statute passed or, if passed in time, to have the law do any good. Packard said, "You leave that to me." We arranged that I would meet him at the Tavern at ten o'clock in the morning of the following day with a written-up proposed bill embodying the suggested provision.

The farmers promoting MILK, Inc., were holding daily meetings in a suite at the Tavern. Packard asked me to explain the proposed bill. I did. All were pleased with the proposed legislation. What followed is a graphic example of the power of Arthur Packard in those days.

He called the chairman of the agricultural committees in both the house and senate and asked them to meet him down at the Tavern and to bring all members of both committees. They responded within an hour. The proposal was explained to and carefully read by each member. The need for it was emphasized by Packard. In his quiet voice he said that the legislators should make it a law immediately.

The committee members went back to the house and senate, arranged the necessary details with the speaker, the lieutenant governor, the president of the senate, and the governor. The bill was introduced under suspension of rules, and under further suspension of rules it went through the house and senate in seventy-two hours, immediately was messaged to the governor, and became law.

I doubt if any legislation in the history of the state was accomplished with a speed equal to that.

True Client Appreciation

The barter system used to be a very common ingredient of the Vermont economic system. Most business was concluded without ever involving the use or exchange of currency. But that was many years ago when Vermont was almost entirely an agricultural society. An interesting holdover of that practice involved my law partner, J. Ward Carver, and his interesting and colorful client, Tony the barber.

Tony was an immigrant from the town of Carrara in Italy, as were many others who came to Barre to work in the granite monumental processing plants after a very special grade of granite was recognized in the hills surrounding Barre. Carrara, as a marble-producing area, gave a kind of training to great numbers of Italians growing up there, which fitted nicely the expanding granite-producing activity in the Barre area that started around 1893 and has continued to this day. These Italian immigrants represented a substantial proportion of the population of Barre City and made substantial contribution to the commercial, social, artistic, and cultural life of that city. They were high-class people. Their second- and third-generation children and grandchildren were outstanding students in our high school and captured a surprisingly large majority of the scholastic honors at Spaulding High School. The Italian women were marvelous cooks, and their homes were immaculate, their children orderly and disciplined, and their family solidity was something to be greatly admired. Eventually these second- and third-generation children came to own and operate skillfully many of the granite plants and other business enterprises in the area, as well as to occupy a large proportion of the professional positions in the community. Barre could never have come to be the bustling, interesting place it is without their outstanding contribution.

Tony was a later immigrant who came not to work in the granite plants but to seek greater opportunity in the place where so many of his relatives and friends had settled. He had learned the barber's trade as an apprentice in Italy. Like many others, however, he had the problem of adjusting to many changes inherent in his new location, not the least of which was to master a new language. But he learned rapidly even though he had problems of pronunciation, as do all who struggle with the language.

Tony and Ward Carver quickly became friends. Their friendship transcended all commercialism and soon drifted into an informal barter arrangement. It developed more by practice than it did by any formal agreement. It was well understood on both sides. Tony was to cut Carver's hair and shave him whenever this service was needed, and Carver was to defend Tony or represent him in any legal matters when those services were needed. Experience showed that Tony got the better of the bargain. Tony needed defending more often than Carver needed his hair cut.

Once Tony got himself involved in a fist fight with another Italian immigrant. Tony came off very much the vic-

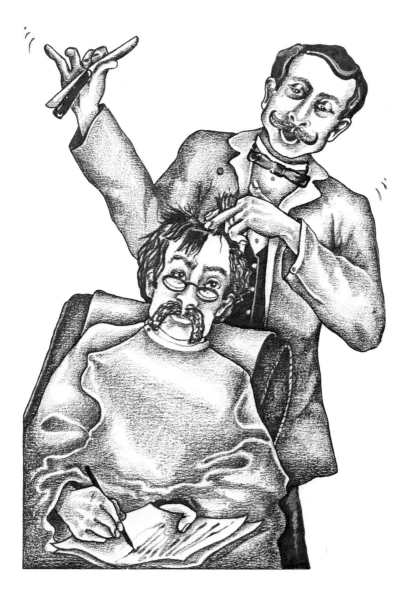

tor. His opponent landed in Barre City Hospital with multiple injuries. While in the hospital Tony's opponent began to worry about his doctor's bills and hospital bills. A well-meaning friend suggested that he should bring suit against Tony for assault and battery. Because Tony had almost none of this world's goods, the wisdom of that advice is open to question.

Eventually, however, suit was brought against Tony. The opponent's lawyer was Joseph Frattini, a capable Italian lawyer in Montpelier, later clerk of the Supreme Court of Vermont. Carver was counsel for Tony in accordance with the barter arrangement. After the testimony was concluded, the usual oral arguments to the jury began. Carver was surprised that Frattini's argument consisted almost entirely of a magnificent portrayal of the many virtues of his client. Not much was said about the evidence. This omission was unusual if, indeed, not irregular. But Carver, who had unusual ability as a forensic lawyer and great capacity for rapid adjustment to surprises, decided to go the plaintiff's counsel one better. So when his turn came he described to the jury in his most articulate manner how greatly Tony's virtues surpassed those of Tony's opponent. Tony, according to Carver, was an almost sainted individual. He was honest, industrious, a good family man, a good churchman, sober, kind, and a generous and dependable citizen. As Carver was making this unusual argument to the jury he occasionally turned to his client sitting at the defendant's table to see how Tony was taking it. Tony was taking it very well. He was smiling and bowing with obvious enjoyment and approval. With every adjective his smile became broader.

In due course the case was submitted to the jury, and in short order the jury returned with a verdict for Tony. To the lawyers in the room this verdict was not wholly unexpected because the evidence quite clearly showed that both parties to the fisticuffs were about equally the aggressor. Hence the judge had instructed the jury that if both were at fault as aggressors then the verdict must be for the defendant.

But these niceties of the law wholly escaped Tony. He interpreted the jury verdict as a quick and complete endorsement of every virtue of his that Carver had described and every adjective Carver had used. Tony was in seventh heaven. And so, after court adjourned, he took occasion to celebrate this great moment of his life and to describe to his friends in the greatest of repetitive detail what had been said of him at the trial. In this celebration he drank copious quantities of a liquid refreshment called "grappa," a homemade product of the grapes of full 100 percent alcoholic content.

That evening, after dinner, Carver had returned to his office to catch up on some of his office work necessarily delayed while in court defending Tony. About nine o'clock Tony came in. He was feeling no pain.

"Meestah Carver, I comea to paya you."

"Tony, you don't owe me anything. Remember our arrangement?"

"Oh, yessa, Mr. Carver, I remember. But disa timea I'ma gonna paya you."

After considerably more of this kind of exchange, Tony drew a roll of bills out of his pocket, began peeling ten-and twenty-dollar bills from the roll, and laid them down tenderly on Carver's desk. All the time he was smiling and nodding. His enjoyment of the verdict had in no measure diminished. After he had laid down $300 he looked at Carver with an adoring expression and said, "Meestah Carver, when you talka I understanda everyting you saya. But when dat Godda Dam Woppa talka I no understanda noting."

Admiration— Not Contempt

I had been retained to assist Gelsie Monti, Esq., in the defense of a criminal prosecution against George Knox, who was charged with having burned his five-ton truck in order to collect the insurance. The trial was held in Orange County Court, Judge Jones presiding. Jones, of course, was not his name. I refrain from using his real name for obvious reasons.

From the start of the trial everything seemed to go wrong. Our client soon created the image of a first-class stinker. So much so that he incurred the hostility of most of those in the courtroom including, most importantly, the judge himself. The judge's feelings were so intense that soon he was flagrantly displaying those feelings in his tone of voice, his gratuitous adverse comments, and his very readable facial expressions. In retrospect, I suppose I could not blame the judge too much, except that a judge is supposed to be able to mask his feelings in the courtroom lest the jury, supposed to be the sole judge of the facts, be adversely influenced. The capacity to do this is a part of what we call judicial temperament.

But, however tolerant I can now be after all these years,

during the trial I was greatly upset. I well knew, even then, that our client was, in fact, a stinker. But he was not on trial for being a stinker. He was on trial for intentionally setting fire to his truck for the purpose of collecting insurance. I was completely convinced that he did not do so. Eventually the jury thought so, too, because they rendered a verdict of not guilty. And even a stinker is entitled to a fair trial.

As the trial progressed, I grew increasingly more angry at the judge's display of prejudice. Finally, I reached the boiling point. With my blood pressure feeling as though it had hit 350, I rose and addressed the court.

"Your Honor," I began, "I have strived mightily to restrain myself during this trial from saying what I am about to say. In fairness to my client I can no longer keep silent. I take violent exception to the conduct of the presiding judge and ask that my exception be noted on the record and the reasons therefor in order that on appeal, if appeal becomes necessary, the Supreme Court should be given a chance to review this tragic exhibition of judicial prejudice and conduct. You, Sir, are a long-time member of the bar in this state. That long service as a lawyer and a judge only serves to make your conduct that much more reprehensible. In all of my experience at the bar I have never seen a more reprehensible exhibition of unjudicial conduct. I regard it as unforgivable conduct and an indication that you are not qualified by temperament to serve in the high office of a Superior Court judge."

As my blood pressure began to subside, I glanced around the courtroom. Expressions of amazement were on the faces of lawyers and court attendants, and Brother Monti was frantically pulling my coattails attempting to make me sit down. Suddenly I realized I was in contempt of court, an offense punishable by jail sentence if the judge in his discretion should so decide.

I watched the judge's countenance. Its expression showed all the colors of the rainbow, beginning with red searing anger, through various shades to a stark white evidencing cold fury. As quietly as I could I stopped talking and sat down. I was sure that I was slated for punishment of the worst kind—probably a period in jail.

For a very long time the judge said not a word. He stared into space, obviously doing some heavy thinking. For what seemed an eternity, one could have heard a pin drop. Finally, in a perfectly cool demeanor the judge addressed the jury:

Gentlemen of the Jury: I am sorry to say that upon sober reflection I want you to know that I think Mr. Davis is completely justified in his intemperate remarks. I apologize to him and I apologize to you. It is the duty of a judge to act at all times in a completely impartial and judicial manner and to refrain from remarks prejudicial to any of the parties to the trial. I have been led astray by my emotions. Most of all, I want to make sure that the rights of this respondent are fully protected. Therefore, Gentlemen of the jury, I charge you to completely obliterate from your mind any prejudicial remarks which I have made in this trial. You are not to hold them against the respondent in any way. Counsel may proceed with the evidence.

You could hear many sighs of relief in the courtroom, most of all mine, as the tension was released by these remarks by the judge.

My "contempt" changed immediately to a tremendous admiration for the judge. It takes a big man to do what he did.

Aiken Story

The capacity for cryptic retort has often been considered a Vermont characteristic. One Vermonter possessing this talent in unusual degree is our former senior senator, the Honorable George D. Aiken. In advocacy, political or otherwise, it can be a powerful tool. In the case of Senator Aiken it may well have been an inherited characteristic, as the following apocryphal story illustrates.

Senator Aiken's father served his state as a member of the Vermont House of Representatives, at one session of which the bill to grant women the right to vote was being considered. Like most important issues in the Vermont legislature, it was hotly contested. Representative Aiken led the forces in favor of the bill. On the third reading he made a powerful speech for the bill. The leader of the opposition then rose and requested permission to interrogate "the member from Putney." Permission was granted, and the exchange went like this:

"Now, Mr. Aiken, if we give women the right to vote, that means we will have to impose upon them all the other duties and responsibilities of citizenship, doesn't it?"

Aiken looked at the ceiling for a moment or two and then answered, "Yes, I suppose so."

"Well, then, Mr. Aiken, that means we will have to make the women serve on juries, too, doesn't it?"

Aiken answered, "Yes, I suppose so."

"Now then, Mr. Aiken, did you know that, in criminal cases in Vermont, juries have to be kept together from the time the case starts until it is finished? Did you know that, Mr. Aiken?"

Aiken's answer was: "Yes, I've heard that is so."

"Now then, Mr. Aiken, let me ask you, supposing your wife was called on a jury, and supposing there were eleven men and one woman, and supposing that case was a criminal case, and supposing it lasted two, three, or four days. How would you like to have your wife kept in a room with eleven men for two, three, or four days and nights? How would you like that, Mr. Aiken?"

After looking at the ceiling for a few seconds, his answer was, "Well, that would depend on who we happened to have for a hired girl!"

An Unequal Contest

During the 1940s I owned and operated a dairy farm on East Hill in Barre Town. During the planting and crop seasons it was necessary to hire extra help. In those days it was still possible to find young men with strong backs, willing hands, and a true farm background who were anxious to earn an extra dollar when opportunity existed. I have never ceased to admire the variety of skills possessed by boys brought up in a farm family on a Vermont dairy farm. These lads never had to "find themselves." They knew where they were and what they were and what life was all about. These boys early in life became great mechanics and good carpenters and could do a fairly good job of blacksmithing, if necessary. They did the painting and repairing not only of all farm buildings as a matter of course but of their wide variety of machinery also. And when they had a problem for which there was no known procedure, they invented one. Their ingenuity was amazing. Farmers had to have those skills, I guess, in order to survive on the farm. But this kind of life built a very special kind of confidence. And out of this confidence came a very special kind of independence of spirit. They did not take kindly to being pushed around, as the following incident portrays.

Of all the young men who worked on my farm Carroll Foster was the most memorable. During World War II he reached draft age and was called up for service. When the war was over and Foster was home he came to call on me. I spent a most interesting evening listening to his experiences as seen through the eyes of a Vermont farm boy. During our conversation I asked him if he got into any kind of trouble while in service.

"Well," said he, somewhat reluctantly, "yes I did, Mr. Davis."

"Do you want to tell me about it, Carroll?" I asked him.

"Sure," he said, "glad to. You see we had a top sergeant who was hard to get along with. Quite a bully he was. I did my best to stand it and did for quite a while. But one day I made the mistake of hitting him. Shouldn't have done it, I know, but he got me pretty mad. So I hit him."

"Did you hurt him any?"

"Oh, a little. I broke his nose and broke his jaw and kind of messed up one of his eyes pretty bad."

"Well, what happened then, Carroll?"

"Oh, they grabbed me and put me in the hoosegow. Didn't mind that too much 'cause of course I knew I shouldn't a hit him. The food wasn't very good, though, and I was a little worried. The next day one of the officers came in to see me. He had a great long sheet of paper. Written on both sides with a typewriter it was. And he sat there and read it to me and then gave it to me."

"What was it, Carroll?" I asked him.

"Well, it was a bunch of charges against me. It told over and over again in sixteen different ways about me hitting the sergeant and how I had broken a whole lot of laws and regulations that I had never even heard of."

"That must have scared you pretty bad, didn't it?"

"Some. Of course I knew I had hit the sergeant. But he bullied me pretty bad and should have been hit. He really pushed me around, Mr. Davis, and nobody ought to have to take that. But I didn't know about all those laws and regulations. And I didn't know just how you go about defending yourself and telling your story in a case like that.

"So, I sat there thinking. And I read the paper again. And again. And then I turned it over and looked on the front. And there it said in great big letters *United States of America* vs. *Carroll Foster.* And I thought about it some more. And I thought how big the United States was and how it had all those armies, navies, battleships, troops, and airplanes. And, by golly, Mr. Davis, I said to myself, I said, 'What a helluva unequal contest this is going to be.'"

A Half Cup Is Better Than a Whole Cup

In the days when the Pavilion Hotel in Montpelier was in its prime, it served a most important state function. Legislators, lobbyists, judges, and witnesses all invariably stayed there. Most political conventions were held in Montpelier, and the participants usually stayed in the hotel while in town. More state business, political and otherwise, was probably transacted in that building than any other in the state including the State House. When the Supreme Court was in session the justices stayed there, as did parties litigant and lawyers with cases before the court. It was traditional for the justices to eat their meals there and to sit at the same table, which was reserved for them in the northwest corner of the dining room. They displayed an august presence when together at that table—equal to that displayed when on the bench in their robes.

One of the judges, whose name shall be forever unknown, had some minor physical problem that caused his physician to restrict his use of coffee. He was told that he could have one cup of coffee per day and only one. And he dearly loved coffee.

At the time in question a new waitress had come to work at the Pavilion. At breakfast on her first day the judge ordered a cup of coffee, which was brought. After drinking it the judge called the waitress over and in his most judicial manner asked her to bring him "a half cup of coffee." The waitress brought him a full cup of coffee and set it down on the table in front of him. He might have felt a sense of guilt for violating his doctor's orders. Perhaps, too, he felt that a half cup of coffee was not another cup of coffee, and hence he would be in technical compliance with his doctor's orders. On the other hand, a full cup would be "more than one." Anyway, he flushed, and speaking again in a most judicial manner but much more emphatically, he addressed the waitress in a voice that was heard throughout most of the room: "Young lady, I ordered a half cup of coffee. Take this cup back to the kitchen and bring me exactly what I ordered—*a half cup of coffee.*"

Every guest in the dining room was watching and listening. The quiet was impressive. The young lady said not a word, picked up the cup, and started for the kitchen. As she reached the swinging doors leading into the kitchen, she paused momentarily and, in a voice likewise heard throughout the dining room, she said, "Doesn't the d——old fool know? He doesn't have to drink only half of it if he doesn't want to!"

A Fish Story

Floyd Mitchell grew up on a farm in Barre Town, graduated from Spaulding High School in Barre City, later was admitted to West Point, graduated with honors, and became an officer in the U.S. Army, where he had a distinguished career. Among other important assignments in the army, he took charge of the mining of the bay off Corregidor Island during World War II. He later lost his life while serving his country in that war.

Whenever he was on leave he would come back to Barre, where he would spend much of his time fishing for trout in the streams around the county, an activity he had loved so much in his boyhood days. On one of these leaves he had been fishing the Nate Smith Brook in Plainfield, Vermont, with much success. His basket contained twenty-four fish, just one short of the twenty-five allowed by law. While patiently angling for that last fish he was accosted by a game warden, who demanded to see his fish. Mitchell willingly complied, and the warden carefully measured every one of the fish. It turned out, according to the warden, that there were two illegal fish out of the twenty-four. One was one-

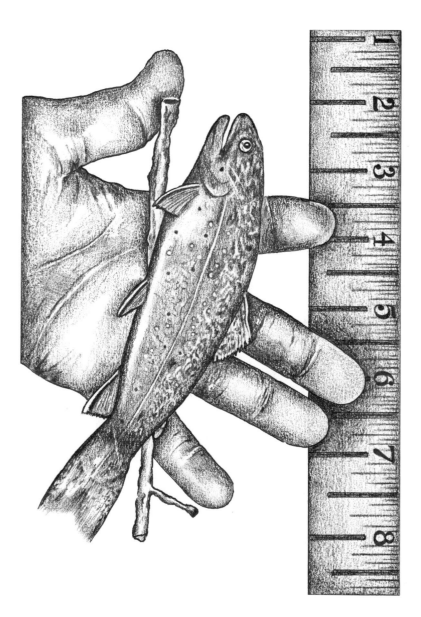

quarter inch and another one-half inch short of the six-inch limit prescribed by law.

Mitchell explained to the warden how he had cut a twig from the branch of a tree before leaving home, had measured it off exactly at six inches, and had carefully measured each fish before putting it in the basket, and that he had caught quite a few short ones, which he had thrown back because they were less than six inches. The warden was unimpressed and eventually swore out a warrant for his arrest, which required his appearance in Barre City Municipal Court. Upon being arraigned in court, Mitchell had pleaded not guilty, bail was fixed at $100, and he was allowed by the judge to be released on his own recognizance, whereupon he came to my office.

After hearing the story I advised Mitchell to plead guilty, explaining that it was after all a minor violation without moral turpitude, and I was sure that the judge would fine him not more than five dollars and costs. But Mitchell was not interested in that kind of a disposition of his case. "I'm not guilty of anything, and I'm not going to say I am." He further explained that, if there was a record of conviction of a criminal offense, it would ultimately find its way onto his army record and might very likely adversely affect his future promotions and assignments in army service.

So, believing him to be sincere and certainly not intentionally committing a crime, I prepared to represent him. Moreover, he was my former schoolmate at Spaulding High School. First, I went to the state's attorney, who was the prosecuting officer, and explained the circumstances of the effect of a conviction on Mitchell's army record. Because this offense was at worst only a minor violation, I asked the state's attorney to exercise his discretion and drop the case. This is a right accorded prosecuting officers. I told him that I was sure that the two fish had shrunk during the hours in the hot sun. But the state's attorney told me that he had discussed the possibility of the fish shrinking with some members of the State Fish and Game Department, and they had assured him that the state would be able to produce a witness from the Biology Department of the University of Vermont who would testify that while fish may shrink sideways, so to speak, they do not and cannot shrink lengthwise because of the nature of their skeletal structure. He refused to drop the case.

I checked with one of the biologists at U.V.M., who told me that it was indeed true that fish do not shrink lengthwise. Puzzling over what to do next, I suddenly remembered a bit of sage advice my father (also a lawyer) had given me in my early years at the bar. I had asked him, "Dad, what do you do when faced by an expert whose testimony, if accepted, will ruin your case?" His answer I have remembered all these years. "Face them right back with another expert," he said. "You'll be surprised how much experts can disagree under the right circumstances." That advice has stood me in good stead many times in later years.

I heard of two brothers living in Woodbury, both in their eighties, who were regarded in the county as the most experienced and knowledgeable fishermen around. I decided that if the state could have a scientific witness expert there was no reason why I couldn't have a practical expert whose expertise was based on experience. So one night after dinner I drove over to Woodbury and had a talk with these two interesting individuals. They had both lived nearly all of their lives as recluses, yet they were obviously voracious readers, and I wondered how their interest had been stimulated in view of the life they had lived.

I explained the case in great detail. I will admit that I

dramatized the horrible results that would follow to Mitchell's army record if he was convicted, and I portrayed the integrity of my client and his noble nature in most glowing terms. Then I said, "And you know all this hangs on a question of whether those two fish could shrink that little bit after four hours in the hot sun." The response was immediate: "You're damn right they shrank," said the older brother.

"But they have an expert biologist from U.V.M. who says fish don't shrink lengthwise," I explained. "Well, By G——, they do shrink. They have on me many times," said the younger brother, giving graphic details of time and place where these things had happened to him. I could feel very keenly their sympathy. Then, after a suitable interval, I cautiously inquired if they would come to Barre and testify to what they had told me. This cooled their enthusiasm some, but, after more discussion about their duty as citizens and the great harm to my client if they failed me, they finally consented. I felt sure that I could get Judge H. William Scott to rule that these two men in their eighties were experts within the meaning of the law because the judge, an ardent fisherman himself, hated the fish and game laws with a passion.

And I was right. He did so rule, to the obvious discomfiture of the state's attorney and the warden. After the presentation of the state's case and their final witness the biologist, I put my client on the stand, who testified briefly in his own defense. Then I put the two Woodbury brothers on. They were fantastic. They had obviously been preparing themselves for this big day by practicing on each other. In colorful, earthy language they told of incident after incident where fish they had caught had shrunk lengthwise in the hot sun. They were doing so well that I began to be afraid they would overdo it. By the time they were through testifying, it was really all over. The jury took less than ten minutes to reach and report their verdict of not guilty.

This case is another example of the profound fact that if you can present a case where the jury *wants* to find in your favor, all you have to do is give them an *excuse* to do so.

A Policeman's Lot Is Not a Happy One

In 1919 I took a year off from law school to earn a little money to pay my expenses for the rest of my college years. I came back from school and got a job with the R.L. Clark Feed Company, which ran a store and sold animal feeds of all kinds to the farmers of the surrounding area and also to many of the residents of the City of Barre. It was quite common in those days for people in Vermont living within city limits to keep chickens, a cow, or even a pig in the backyard. Zoning was completely unheard of then.

Much of the business of the feed store consisted of supplying feed in small lots to these domestic animals. Usually the orders were delivered by the store, for which the store kept a large three-ton truck and a horse and express wagon. My job was to drive the truck and assist an older and more experienced man in making these deliveries. This man was James Sullivan, a large, hearty, genial Irishman whom everybody loved and who knew the city intimately and nearly everybody in it.

Across the street from the store was a small colony of Lebanese people, some of whom kept chickens. They soon learned, and so did the chickens, that the best and cheapest way to feed the chickens was to let them find their way across the street to the store premises, where they could pick up a good living from grain that would be scattered around while being handled. Adjacent to the store itself we had a large building called the engine house, where carloads of grain in one-hundred-pound bags were stored after being unloaded from the freight cars. Some of these chickens would find their way into the engine house and satisfy their hunger there. In doing so, they were often so inconsiderate as to leave their droppings on the bags. Because it was always a little dark in the engine house both Jim and I would sometimes get our hands into these messes when we went to pick up a bag or two. It was always an annoying experience, to say the least.

Complaints to the police department and resulting warnings to the Lebanese colony produced no results. So, in order to educate the Lebanese people to keep their chickens at home, we sometimes would shut the door when we discovered a good fat rooster in the engine house, catch him, put him in a bran sack, throw him onto the truck, and, on the next trip out with deliveries, we would sell him to some butcher along the route. We kept the money from these occasional sales in a separate fund to buy candy with which to restore our flagging energies. We called it the "Education and Welfare Fund." Jim taught me this little exercise, as he was the one that started it originally, long before I came to work at Clark's.

Everything went well until a traumatic event occurred. A new mayor was elected. One of his first official acts was to appoint Jim Sullivan as the new chief of police. At first almost everyone thought that the new mayor had lost his mind. Sullivan had had no preparation or experience for or with police work whatsoever. But this appointment turned out to be one of the wisest things the mayor did while he was in office. Jim became one of the best chiefs of police the city ever had. He served with distinction for many years and gave complete satisfaction to the citizens of Barre. He had an uncanny knack for the job. His methods were not sophisticated but most successful. His system of crime detection was based on a combination of a remarkable capacity for common sense and his thorough knowledge of almost every person in the city. And everybody loved him, which helped. When a crime was committed he would make a preliminary investigation; he would sit down and ask himself, "Now, who would commit a crime like this?" After a bit of pondering he would come up with the correct answer in a surprisingly large proportion of his cases.

A few days after Sullivan had taken up his new duties I came across a big fat rooster in the engine room. Having been well trained, I slammed the door, caught him, and put him in a sack. On my next trip to the North End of Barre I spied Jose Cano's roan horse and wagon beside the curb in front of the pool hall where Jose often whiled away the time. Cano was a local butcher, with whom both Sullivan and I had sometimes done business before. I stopped the truck, rousted Cano out of the pool hall, sold him the rooster for a $1.50, and deposited the money in the "Education and Welfare Fund" as usual.

Unknown to me, as it later appeared, this rooster belonged to Mary John, an aggressive member of the Lebanese colony. This particular rooster was her pride and joy. About the time I sold the rooster Mrs. John was visiting a friend farther down in the North End. Upon completing her visit she started to walk home. Her course took her up North Main Street. Upon arriving opposite the pool hall, she was shocked to see the head and neck of her pride and joy sticking up through the slats of a chicken crate in the express wagon.

At that time the state's attorney for Washington County was Earle R. Davis, who also happened to be my father. Mrs. John knew my father, so she hurried to his office and made her complaint. After listening to her story my father sent for Jose Cano. Upon being questioned Cano promptly admitted buying the rooster but refused to tell from whom he had bought it. After much questioning and being threatened with jail for his refusal, all he would say was, "It was a good friend of yours and a good friend of mine." Frustrated and puzzled, my father sent for Sullivan, the new chief of police. After hearing the story, Jim suggested that the matter be turned over to him for investigation. He said he was confident that he could solve the mystery.

A couple of hours later, after delivering all the orders on my truck, I was winging my way back up Main Street heading for the store. As I rounded the corner from Main Street onto Prospect Street, I noticed our new chief of police, who seemed to be watching for something or somebody. He was resplendent in his new uniform, which, with his rosy countenance and silver gray hair, made him look not only handsome but very official, too. He stepped out from the curb, flagged me down, and came to the window of the cab.

"How much did you get for that rooster you sold to Jose Cano?" he asked.

"What rooster?" I replied with what I hoped was an innocent countenance.

"Don't give me any of that lip, young man," he replied. "You may be able to fool some people but you can't fool me. So don't try. I want to know how much you got."

Well, things began to look a bit serious. But, what a change. Here was the man who had taught me the technique of supporting the Education and Welfare Fund—my erstwhile friend and coconspirator—now religiously acting the part of an honest and determined police officer. I tried my best to keep a straight face, but it was just impossible. In spite of myself I burst out laughing.

"A dollar and fifty cents," I replied.

"O.K. Give me the money."

So I gave him the $1.50. He took it back to Cano, retrieved the rooster, and delivered it back to Mrs. John, who thereupon was ecstatic and dropped her complaint.

Thus was justice done.

My father's reaction was, "I hope you learned something."

Judge Moulton and the Bus

Judge Moulton was a most able and distinguished judge. He served many years on the Superior Court bench and later became a member of the Supreme Court and eventually its chief justice. He was a great scholar, and his opinions as chief justice of the Supreme Court contained in the official *Vermont Reports* were in many cases literary gems. But he was also a very dignified man—dignified in speech and bearing and even in the way he was attired.

The Vermont Transit Lines, which now serves so much of the state and parts of New England, was originally started by a Mr. Jewett of Waterbury. In the beginning it consisted of one bus that traveled up the eastern side of the state and then through Montpelier on to Burlington. It was driven most of the time by Mr. Jewett himself, who never really looked the part of a transportation magnate.

Judge Moulton never drove a car and relied on the bus for transportation from Burlington to Montpelier and return. One day, as the bus pulled up in front of the Pavilion Hotel to discharge and take on passengers, it appeared that there was only standing room for the first few who boarded the bus.

The judge was somewhat irritated. Speaking to the driver, who was Mr. Jewett, the owner, the judge said, "This is a disgrace. If I were running a bus company I would have equipment enough to accommodate the public."

Promptly answered Mr. Jewett, "If I were a Supreme Court Justice of Vermont I would be driving my own car."

A Short-Time Tourist

The town meeting, as a mechanism for political decision and action, has been a cherished institution since Vermont became an independent state in 1791. Nowhere has it been defended more fiercely nor endured so long. In view of the present preoccupation with "regionalism," the adherents of the town meeting system may soon fight their fiercest battle for survival. If they lose, something of unique value, intangible but substantial, will disappear from Vermont life.

The town meeting, whatever its merits or demerits, did give all citizens a sense of participation. Many a citizen learned the art of rough-and-tumble political debate and sometimes disclosed capacity for leadership where it was least suspected.

The Town of Stowe, once a prosperous agricultural township within an agricultural county, bore little resemblance to the present glamorous ski resort. It is interesting to note that, in spite of these profound changes in people, occupation, and physical environment, Stowe has not greatly diminished interest in, or use of, this democratic method to settle important local issues. The following story

161

has been handed down from "the old days."

The issue was the building of a new schoolhouse. Debate waxed hot and heavy. Finally, Mr. Brown, the leader of the opposition, addressed the moderator.

"Mr. Moderator, may I have permission to interrogate Mr. Smith?" (Mr. Smith was the leader of the proponents.) Permission being granted, the exchange went like this:

"Mr. Smith, how long have you lived in Vermont?"

"Thirty years."

"How long have you lived in Stowe?"

"Thirty years."

Thereupon, Mr. Brown, with a contented sigh, turned to the moderator and said, "Mr. Moderator, I don't think we need to be told how to run our business by any goldarned tourist!"

A U.S. Attorney General
Is Hired

I am indebted to the late Fred Howland for the following incident. It will be remembered that after Calvin Coolidge had been elected president there was a scandal involving the then attorney general, which resulted in his resignation. Coolidge presented several names of distinguished American lawyers, one after the other, to the Senate for ratification, and one by one they were turned down by the Senate. Finally, in desperation, Coolidge turned to his old Vermont schoolmate and friend, John Garibaldi Sargent, whose great ability and integrity were known throughout New England. The circumstances under which Sargent was asked by the president to assume that office I am sure are not well known.

Sargent was visiting his old friend Howland in the latter's office at National Life Insurance Company when a call came through to the switchboard operator. The person making the call asked if Mr. Sargent was at this number. The National Life switchboard operator then asked, "Who is this?" The answer was, "This is the personal secretary to the president of the United States." The operator, suspicious of a practical joke replied, "Is that so? This is Joan of Arc." Shortly, she

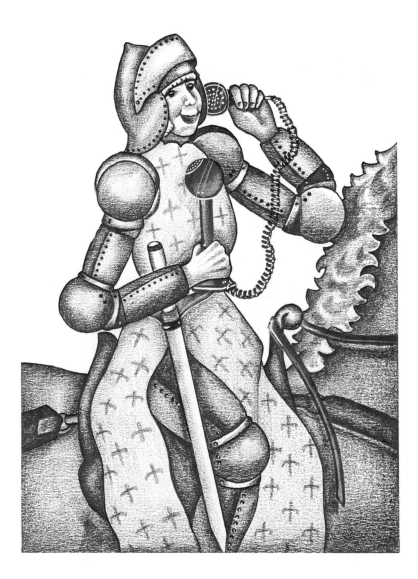

was covered with confusion when she found that it indeed was the secretary of the president of the United States. Hasty inquiry was made and Sargent was found in Howland's office, and the president was put on the line with Sargent.

"Hello, Gary," said the president, "this is Cal."

"Oh, hello, Cal, what can I do for you?"

"Well, you can do me a good favor, if you will."

"What's that?" said Sargent.

"I want you to come down and be my attorney general," said the president.

"Oh, God, I couldn't do that, Cal."

"But I really need you, Gary," said the president.

"Well, if you really need me maybe I could. Wish you'd find somebody else, though."

"No, I want you, Gary, and I need you badly," said the president.

"Well, all right, when do you want me?" asked Gary.

"I'd like you to come the first of the week," said the president.

"Oh, God, I couldn't do that," he replied.

"Why not?" asked the president.

"I've got a lot of cases in Windsor County Court, and the Jury cases are on right now."

"When could you come, Gary?"

"Two weeks at the earliest," he replied.

"Well, if that's the best you can do I guess that's what it'll have to be," said the president.

"All right Cal. I'll be there. Take care of yourself, Cal. Good-bye."

Six Brief Cases

The Motter

One of the divorce cases that came before the Windham County Court while I was presiding involved a couple in their eighties who had not been married very long. The petitioner was the husband. At the time this case was heard the grounds for divorce under Vermont law were less inclusive than they now are. Hence many cases in those days were tried on allegations of "intolerable severity." Intolerable severity meant physical abuse or mental cruelty of a kind sufficient to endanger the health of the aggrieved party.

The petitioner was testifying to a rather long list of abuses by his aged wife. Among them he included an instance of physical abuse that puzzled me for a moment. He said that his wife had hit him over the head with a "motter."

"Would you repeat that, Sir?" I asked the petitioner.

"A motter," said the petitioner again.

Observing that I did not quite understand, he tried to be helpful. "A motter, Judge, don't you know what a motter is? One of those things that hangs on the wall—'God Bless Our Home.'"

A Distasteful Chore

John Perkins, my farmer neighbor on East Hill in Barre, received his income tax form from the Treasury Department and, like most of us, put off the disagreeable task of filing it until the last moment. In his case he gradually gathered all the memoranda and data off the walls of the cow stable, notes pinned up in the kitchen, and loose papers spread around in several drawers in his rolltop desk, and he finally got everything together the night before the last day to send the form in.

He was not in a happy mood as he approached the task of making up the form. It was Saturday night, when he and Mrs. Perkins usually went to town to a movie. He opened the form, scowled at it, and noticed in the upper right-hand corner a rectangular block in black ink that said, "DO NOT WRITE IN THIS SPACE." It fully reflected his mood and his spirit when he boldly wrote, "I'LL WRITE WHERE I DAMN PLEASE."

She Didn't Know

The respondent was accused of rape, one element of which is, of course, the lack of consent on the part of the complainant. The complainant, an attractive but not overly bright girl of twenty years, was testifying to the details.

Among other things, the state claimed that after the episode eighty dollars in currency that had been tucked under the complainant's stocking was found to be missing, with the implication that the respondent had added injury to insult by stealing the money.

As the girl reached the point in her story where she was telling of the "tempestuous wooing" by the respondent, she was asked the necessary question to show lack of consent.

Said the state's attorney, "Didn't you make any objection to this conduct on the part of the respondent?"

"But I didn't know he was going to rob me."

An Aid to Memory

Judge Rowell was a distinguished and scholarly judge of the old school. Soon after Joe Frattini took up his duties as clerk of the Supreme Court he was walking down the street with the judge at noon recess right after a succession of lengthy arguments by counsel in the Supreme Court.

"Judge," said Joe, "could I ask you a question?"

"Of course, Jobie. What is it?"

"I would just like to ask you if you judges actually remember what these lawyers have said when they make these long arguments?"

"Well, Jobie," answered the judge, "you see, it's like this. If it's awfully good we sometimes remember. If it's awfully bad we never forget."

A Good Argument

One of the subjects that keeps recurring in the legislature of Vermont is the question of providing a governor's home, or Mansion, as it is called in most states. Vermont is one of only three or four states that do not provide a home for the Governor while in office. There are good arguments on both sides of the question, although my opinion is that, if Vermont were to have one, it should be a modest but dignified home rather than a pretentious structure as most states build.

Sitting in the gallery of the House of Representatives

some years ago, I remember the debate on the third reading of a bill that proposed such a home. The argument that clinched the fate of the bill in the negative came from a farmer from the northern part of the state, who said simply, "Mr. Speaker and Members of the House, I don't think we have to spend money we ain't got for somethin' we don't need."

A Model Charge

The judge's charge to the jury is supposed to be an exposition of the law applicable to the facts presented by the witnesses. It is supposed to be an aid to the jury in the performance of its duty. Too often such charges are too long and too complicated and serve more to confuse than to clarify. The following charge cannot be said to offend in that respect.

It was given by the Vermont justice of the peace who, with a jury, was trying a small automobile damage case in which I was attorney for the defendant:

Gentlemen of the jury: I am now supposed to tell you what the law is. It's very simple. It's like this. If you believe what the plaintiff has testified to and the plaintiff's witnesses, and what the plaintiff's lawyer said in argument, why, you will give a verdict for the plaintiff. If you believe the defendant and the defendant's witnesses and what the defendant's lawyer said in argument, why, you will find a verdict for the defendant.

Then, pausing to expectorate expertly into the spitoon, he continued: "But if you believe as I do, I don't know what in H—— you will do."

A Matter of Economy

One of Vermont's unique institutions is the office of assistant judge, colloquially called the "side judge." This institution was originally borrowed from the Pennsylvania Constitution. Pennsylvania, and every other state that had such an office or one similar to it, has long since done away with it. The "side judge" is an elective officer, and two are elected in each county. They are uniformly not lawyers. However, they have equal authority with the Superior Court judge, who is the presiding officer of the three-member court.

In a few instances the two lay judges have overruled the presiding judge, even on questions of law. One interesting case came from Bennington County, where two lay judges overruled the presiding judge, who was a lawyer, on a legal question. The case went to Supreme Court and the lay judges were sustained!

By and large, however, the assistant judges do not attempt to exercise their authority on matters of law but do take a part in the sentencing of convicted respondents in criminal cases, fixing bail, and handling procedural matters of that kind.

The reason for "side judges" in those early days was the fear of authority. In those days the prevailing philosophy was to divide up all kinds of power among judicial, executive, and legislative and then to provide further checks and balances in countless situations so that no one person would become possessed of dictatorial authority.

The reason the institution has remained so long in Vermont is that the assistant judges are provided for in the state Constitution, and therefore the office cannot be discontinued without an amendment to the Constitution, with all its attendant delays and difficulties. Periodically, however, an attempt is made in the legislature to remove the office from the constitutional provisions. Some years ago such an attempt was made, with the following colloquy.

The sponsor of the bill, on the third reading, made an impassioned plea to get rid of the office of assistant judge by providing for a referendum to be submitted to the voters to amend the Constitution. Winding up his eloquent plea, he said, "These assistant judges are perfectly useless. Moreover, they are a great expense. Why, we might just as well carve a couple of 'side judges' out of basswood and set them up there on the bench and save the money."

Just about that time a member from a remote section of the state, who had been overimbibing in one of Montpelier's kitchen dives during the noon hour, was taking his seat. Immediately he arose, somewhat unsteadily, and addressed the Speaker: "Mr. Speaker, I resent that statement. I don't think we have to spend money carving our 'side judges' out of basswood. The ones we've got are just as good as that."

He Didn't Want To

A reputation for longevity used to be, and still is, attributed to lifelong Vermonters. A couple from New Jersey, interested in exploring Vermont, were advised to cover the back roads and talk with the natives. This they did for a solid week.

On one occasion, in mid-July, they came to a beautiful little farmstead and, beside the road, saw a middle-aged Vermonter diligently sawing wood with a bucksaw. After a nice chat with the Vermonter, the husband of the New Jersey couple said, "My, it's hot. I don't think you ought to be out here sawing wood like this in this 85° weather. Incidentally, how old are you, if you don't mind?"

"Sixty-five."

"Well, of course, sixty-five is not very old, but still, you shouldn't be out here in such hot weather engaging in such strenuous physical exercise."

"I know. But I have to get this wood sawed this morning because I have to go over this afternoon and help my father get in the hay on the south meadow.

"You have a father?"

"Oh, yes, I have a father."

"How old is he?"

"Eighty-five."

"Well, for heaven's sake! Vermonters sure live to good ripe old ages. But neither of you should be working so hard in such weather."

"I know, but Dad and I have to get this hay in this afternoon because tonight we have to go to my grandfather's wedding."

"You have a grandfather still living?"

"Yes."

"How old is he?"

"A hundred and five."

"A hundred five! For heaven's sake, why does he want to get married?"

"He doesn't *want* to."

A Vermont Perspective

Professor Allen Foley, long-time distinguished professor of history at Dartmouth College, lived in Norwich, Vermont. As close as he was to the New Hampshire line, he was nevertheless a Vermonter through and through. He had a wide reputation as a collector and raconteur of Vermont humor. His book on Vermont humor is widely read and gives chuckles to Vermonters and non-Vermonters alike.

After his retirement from Dartmouth College, he served several terms as representative to the General Assembly from his home district. A bill, which was somewhat controversial, would permit Vermont towns to elect a nonresident as one of their listers. The motive behind the bill was to help some of the small resort towns get some expertise from part-time residents of the town who were engaged in the real estate business in their states of residence. On the third reading a roll call was called for. After the vote the house adjourned for lunch. Allen's seatmate, a great friend of Allen's, followed him down the aisle.

"Allen," he said, "I noticed that you voted for that bill."

"Yes," said Allen. "Why do you ask?"

"Well," said the seatmate, "my constituents aren't going to like it."

"Why not?" asked Allen. "It is purely voluntary. You don't have to do it unless you want to."

"Yes, I know," said the seatmate, "but my constituents aren't going to want anybody else to have the right to do something that they don't want to do."

A New Experience

One of the pleasant fringe benefits available to a governor of Vermont is the frequent opportunity to crown queens—Ski Queens, Snow Queens, Dairy Queens, Maple Sugar Queens, Carnival Queens, and just plain beauty queens. They are invariably beautiful and attractive young ladies with sparkling personalities, and the audiences always seem to enjoy the event almost as much as the winner.

When I went to Brattleboro to crown the Carnival Queen, I was invited to stay overnight with one of my old-time lawyer friends, Osmer Fitts, and his gracious wife, Dorothy.

Next door to their home lived a ten-year-old lad who knew the Fitts family well, and he had heard a rumor that the governor was staying at their home that night. So he came over to see his friend, Osmer, and run down the real facts.

"Is it true, Mr. Fitts, that the governor is going to stay with you and Mrs. Fitts tonight?"

"Yes, it is," replied Osmer. "Why do you ask?"

"Gee, Mr. Fitts, do you suppose I could meet the governor? I would love to meet the governor."

"OK," said Osmer. "Now you just be out there tomorrow morning over by the garage, and when the governor leaves you'll have a chance to meet him."

Sure enough, at eight o'clock in the morning when I came out to leave for Montpelier a bright-eyed ten-year-old was waiting. He had with him one of the most beautiful black Labrador dogs I had ever seen. The relationship between dog and boy was beautiful to behold. We were introduced by Osmer and had a short but interesting chat, and then I drove away to return to Montpelier.

A week or ten days later Osmer was in Montpelier on business and while there made a point of coming to my office for a short visit. He was chuckling when he came in.

"What's so funny, Ozzie?" I asked.

"Well, you remember my neighbor lad you met when you stayed with us last week? After you left he turned to me and said, 'Thank you, Mr. Fitts. Thank you, thank you. I just can't thank you enough. You know, this is the first time my dog ever met a governor!'"

813

Davis, Deane C.

Justice in the Mountains.

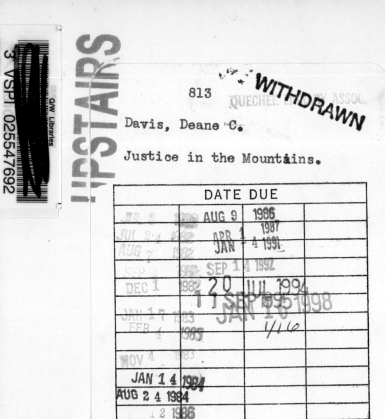

DATE DUE			
	AUG 9	1986	
JUL 2 4 1982	APR 1	1987	
AUG 7 1982	JAN 4 1991		
SEP 1982	SEP 1 4 1992		
DEC 1 1982	2 0 JUL 1994		
	1 1 SEP 1995 1998		
JAN 1 7 1983	JAN 1 6		
FEB 4 1983	1/16		
NOV 4 1983			
JAN 1 4 1984			
AUG 2 4 1984			
1 2 1986			

CROSSCURRENTS *Modern Critiques*

CROSSCURRENTS *Modern Critiques*
Harry T. Moore, *General Editor*

Warren French

The Social Novel

AT THE END OF AN ERA

WITH A PREFACE BY

Harry T. Moore

Carbondale and Edwardsville

SOUTHERN ILLINOIS UNIVERSITY PRESS

FEFFER & SIMONS, INC.

London and Amsterdam

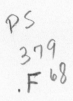

For my Mother,
Mrs. Helen W. French

FIRST PUBLISHED, FEBRUARY 1966
SECOND PRINTING, MAY 1967

PREFACE

WARREN FRENCH, who teaches at the University of Missouri at Kansas City, has written books on Frank Norris, John Steinbeck, and J. D. Salinger and has edited A Companion to "The Grapes of Wrath," a valuable and well-documented study of the Dust Bowl, the "Okies," and other phenomena of the thirities. Now, in The Social Novel at the End of an Era, he revisits that troubled decade, looking at the work of several novelists.

He offers some surprises. He does not, for example, deal with any of the group of writers of the so-called proletarian school, and he does not (except in passing) take up the work of one of the notable social novelists of the period, James T. Farrell, who wrote of the Irish middle class in Chicago. Rather unexpectedly, Mr. French examines a book by William Faulkner and one by Ernest Hemingway. John Steinbeck would of course be anticipated, and Mr. French gives us a fresh view of The Grapes of Wrath (In Dubious Battle, Steinbeck's other outstanding social novel, receives only incidental mention). Mr. French also grants consideration to the pair of novels, now little known, which in 1939 shared the American Booksellers' Award with The Grapes of Wrath: Dalton Trumbo's Johnny Got His Gun and Elgin Groseclose's Ararat. There is also a discussion of Robert Penn Warren's Night Rider (1938), a story of the Kentucky "tobacco wars" of the early twentieth century.

Much of this, then, is new ground, terrain not covered in other studies of the social novel. Mr. French begins with a useful survey of the end of the era—between-wars period—mentioned in the title of this book. It was at the close of this period that Faulkner, Hemingway, and Steinbeck brought out the novels Mr. French explores in the main part of his study: The Hamlet, For Whom the Bell Tolls, and The Grapes of Wrath. He provides a thorough background for the study of each of them.

Faulkner is much else, but he is a social novelist, especially in The Hamlet. Mr. French, who from 1948 to 1950 taught at the University of Mississippi, is well acquainted with Faulkner's state and home town. In providing background material for The Hamlet, Mr. French looks at the careers of Senators Vardaman and Bilbo and of Congressman Rankin—relevantly, as the reader will see, for after consulting this expertly documented account, he will have a much fuller acquaintance than before with the Snopeses and their contemporaries. When Mr. French comes to The Grapes of Wrath, he not only analyses the social forces that motivate the story, but he also presents a most interesting discussion of the historical agrarian idealism which underlies it. In the case of For Whom the Bell Tolls, he shifts his focus from the purely American scene to take up the prophetically viewed troubles of an American in "A Troubled World."

This is a distinctly individualized book; I don't know any other that is quite like it. As I said earlier, it covers new terrain. I think that all students and readers of the modern novel, and of the modern American novel in particular, will find this study stimulating.

Now and then I differ with Mr. French, as almost everyone disagrees with parts of any book of this kind; I have elsewhere expressed myself about what I consider some of the limitations of The Grapes of Wrath and For Whom the Bell Tolls. Mr. French says the reason for my attitude is that I am interested primarily in "artistic" novels. That may well be, but I certainly served an apprenticeship to the social novel, and was writing publicly about Steinbeck when Mr. French was in high school. Today I read social novels as eagerly as any other kind—when they are good. Proust certainly wrote a social novel, and that is what the Russians (some of whom are pretty good) turn out regularly. Some of the newer German work—of Heinrich Böll, Günter Grass, and Uwe Johnson—is social as well as symbolical. There is nothing wrong with the genre itself, which can be fairly inclusive, as Mr. French shows. In reading what he says about Hemingway's Spanish-war novel, my respect for that book has increased somewhat. Nothing is likely to make me care very much for The Grapes of Wrath, which seems to me full of sentimentality and quackery, however much the author "means well." But even those who don't care for that book must admit that it is a milestone in the history of the American social novel; and we inevitably teach it in our courses. Mr. French's projection of the background of this novel, as of the others he discusses here, remains highly valuable.

I for one am extremely glad that he wrote this book, and I hope that other readers will feel likewise.

HARRY T. MOORE

Southern Illinois University
September 6, 1965

ACKNOWLEDGMENTS

MUCH OF Chapter Two has appeared in altered form in the Fall, 1964, issue of the *Midcontinent American Studies Journal,* under the title "The Background of Snopesism in Mississippi Politics."

This book grows out of a seminar in American fiction during the 1930's that I conducted at Kansas State University in the fall of 1963. I am grateful to the dozen graduate students whose questions directed my research, and most especially to Mrs. Laura Greene, who remained interested enough in the project to read the completed manuscript.

After Professor Harry Moore suggested that I write this book, a generous research grant from the College of Arts and Sciences of Kansas State University made it possible for me to spend the summer of 1964 in Madison, Wisconsin, collecting materials and organizing the presentation. I particularly wish to thank the libraries of the University of Wisconsin and the Wisconsin State Historical Society for granting me the use of their facilities.

W. F.

CONTENTS

The Social Novel

AT THE END OF AN ERA

1 THE END OF AN ERA

A LONG-SICK WORLD died a protracted and agonizing death between March 15, 1939, and June 15, 1940. These dates are not arbitrary. On March 15, 1939, troops of Nazi Germany, Hungary, and Romania occupied what the Munich arrangements had left of independent Czechoslovakia, thus irrevocably destroying British Prime Minister Neville Chamberlain's wistful hope that Hitler's ambitions could be contained by appeasement and that there might be "peace in our time." Fifteen months later, on June 15, 1940, Paris fell to Hitler's mechanized hordes.

The actual declaration of war on September 3, 1939, following German moves against Poland, was but one of a series of incidents that the rape of Czechoslovakia had made inevitable. Not until the fall of Paris, nine and a half months later, was it driven home to a world whose sickness had been evasion and self-delusion that its end had come. It would be hard to overemphasize both the actual and symbolic significance of the German occupation of Paris, for the "city of light" had been the fashionable and cultural capital not just of France but of the whole now prostrate democratic world. The city's significance was caught best, not in pompous political pronouncements that followed the French collapse, but in the sentimental lyrics of Jerome Kern and Oscar Hammerstein II's popular song, "The Last Time I Saw Paris." Borrowing their title for a book of reminiscences whose uncommon popularity showed how the fall of Paris had moved even the remote American public, Elliott Paul, one of the most diehard expatriates, summed up in his last chapter the meaning of a fateful day.

> In future years will always be remembered the day of the black rain, when all those who could or would had fled, and the others were waiting. Some said it was because of oil from blown-up tanks and others believed it might be a deadly gas sent by the Germans. A few thought and tens of thousands hoped it was the end of the world.
>
> It was the end of a world in which Paris was supreme, in which France was alive, in which there was a breath of freedom. There was oil in the blackened air, and soot in the rain, and the wretched city was pressed upon by the lowering sky. Greasy buildings, empty. Dingy pavements, bare.[1]

When had this era that ended in the black rain begun? We have become accustomed to regarding the two dizzying decades of boom-and-bust between two world wars as a unique entity. As passing years, however, give us greater perspective on the history of our own time, we begin to recognize that the years between 1919 and 1939 were simply those in which seed sown earlier bore deadly fruit. Even the protracted and ghastly first World War was but an uncompleted episode that delayed rather than averted the end. What we still, now somewhat anachronistically, call "modern history" can most meaningfully be said to have begun also in Paris on March 1, 1871: on that occasion conquering Germans entered the city to symbolize their victory in the Franco-Prussian War. The humiliating peace that ended this struggle consolidated the German Empire, led to the establishment of the Third French Republic, and defined the power struggle that would culminate in the blitzkrieg of 1940.

Few years have seen such important changes in the Western world as those around 1870. With the consolidation of a host of petty states into the modern kingdoms of Italy and Germany, the abolition of slavery and the establishment of the principle of the indissoluble union in the United States, the abolition of serfdom in Russia, and the elimination of the Vatican as a temporal political power with the absorption of the Roman States into Italy, four of the most influential hangovers from the Middle Ages had at last been eliminated at the very time that new inventions and improving industrial techniques vastly increased Western productive capacity.

The industrialization and centralization of the European economy spurred a new drive to control both sources of raw materials and captive markets for manufactured goods. England, France, Spain had already held and largely lost vast colonial empires. The Monroe Doctrine and Napoleon III's misadventure in Mexico discouraged dreams of re-establishing European political control of the Americas. The dynamic nations, prattling about "the white man's burden," turned, therefore, with new vigor to the division of heretofore generally inaccessible Africa and the South Seas and a less successful effort to appropriate China. While European nations had for centuries held stations on the African coast, the parceling out of the mysterious interior did not get fully underway until Germany and Italy were able to join France, England, and Belgium in grubstaking claims.

Concurrently with this change in the political complexion of the Western world, two important new doctrines had assumed the character of modern religions in providing motivation and direction for the change. Darwin's fastidiously scientific theories about natural selection and "the survival of the fittest" were vulgarized into a new defense for laissez-faire policies and predatory economic imperialism, while the Utopian dreams of library-haunting Karl Marx were to provide illiterate "have-nots" with their most effective rallying cry in a world of imperialist exploitation.

Casting about for a convenient label for this Age of Paris

in the history books of the future, one is struck by the pertinence of the word *irresponsible*. There had been irresponsible ages and rulers before, of course, but never had irresponsibility been able to manifest itself on such a global scale as during the nineteenth-century search for plunder and the twentieth-century convulsions over the distribution and management of this plunder. This irresponsibility reached its horrifying climax in the negotiations after the first World War, during which European powers sought to evade obligations accepted under pressure and the United States turned its back on the League of Nations, which offered the sole faint hope for preventing the repetition of past mistakes on a more cataclysmic scale, because our nation felt that it could retain its chastity only by shunning depraved foreigners and practicing a repressive prohibition at home.

The perfect symbols for this age of irresponsibility are the self-ordained aristocrats in F. Scott Fitzgerald's *The Great Gatsby*, who, as narrator Nick Carraway says, "retreated into their vast carelessness and left others to clean up the mess that they had made," while dreamers like Gatsby found only disillusionment and death awaiting them. In 1939 those remnants of the West that had not succumbed to some form of authoritarianism awoke at last to discover that with Czechoslovakia gone and Spain gone, too, a few days later, evasions eventually caught up with one and one must either accept responsibilities or capitulate to ruthless totalitarianism.

The decision to resist came nearly too late—had come too late defeatists suspected in the black days of 1940. Over nearly all the serious fiction of the late thirties hangs the overpowering shadow of the conviction that Paris and the world it provided with a cultural focal point would not rise again. Even the popular Kern and Hammerstein song spoke of remembering rather than regaining the lost world. The incredible defense of Britain, Hitler's staggering miscalculation in dividing his forces to attempt to subjugate Russia, the defeat of the fascist powers, and the subsequent fumbling attempts to move toward a new world under a threat of atomic destruction that could not be swept under the rug were in the unforeseeable future when the books that I will discuss were written, and about all of these books is an air of threnody for "civilized" man.

During the last days of this era of what seemed the suicide of individualism, each of three great American novelists, who have subsequently shared the supreme international distinction of winning the Nobel Prize, published one of his most ambitious novels. Curiously, the growing perspective of a quarter of a century allows us to see that in *The Hamlet, The Grapes of Wrath*, and *For Whom the Bell Tolls*, Faulkner, Steinbeck, and Hemingway made their outstanding contribution to the social novel.

This term, "social novel," needs explanation because almost all fiction dramatizes the relationship between the individual and society, and there is no accepted definition for the term. Generally, it has been applied to novels with a purpose or thesis, but again it is difficult to imagine a serious—or even readable—novel without some controlling thesis. In order to focus upon a specially interesting group of novels, I use the term in a very limited sense. By "social novel," I mean a work that is so related to some specific historical phenomena that a detailed knowledge of the historical situations is essential to a full understanding of the novel at the same time that the artist's manipulation of his materials provides an understanding of why the historical events involved occurred. The events may, like those connected with the Spanish Civil War or the Okie migration, be specifically indentifiable, or they may be invented to typify kinds of occurrences like strikes or lynchings that pose grave social problems.

The event need not have occurred close to the time of the writing if the novel deals—like Robert Penn Warren's

Night Rider—with a force—like twentieth-century terrorist groups—still active when the novel appeared, especially if the novelist (like Warren) draws upon a background of his own experiences. I am not concerned, however, with that diverting anomaly, the "historical novel," which purports to re-create the surface appearance of the glamorous past. Nor do I consider the kind of case study like the Utopian novel [2] in which an unlikely tale is concocted to communicate the author's vision of the good society. The novels I treat are most likely to be confused with such plump clannish chronicles as Stephen Longstreet's hard-bound soap opera *Decade: 1929–1939*, in which the interminable petty bickerings of a self-centered family are occasionally interrupted by cries like, "Goodness, the market has crashed!" or "I see poor Austria has been raped by the Nazi beast," to lend an unwarranted air of social history.

The novels that I will discuss are rather of special interest, not only to literary enthusiasts, but also—as Nelson M. Blake points out—to social scientists and anyone else interested in deepening his knowledge of the world.[3] When these novels are read in conjunction with histories of the period they portray, the two kinds of work shed reciprocal light on each other and deepen our awareness that truth cannot be glimpsed from a single perspective.

There is likely to be little quarrel that *The Grapes of Wrath* is both Steinbeck's grandest achievement and one of the outstanding works of social fiction of its era, however we define "social novel" and limit the era. A best seller for two years after its publication, this saga of dispossessed Oklahomans seeking a new start against overwhelming odds in California has, unlike most best sellers, remained one of the most widely read works of American fiction. Despite some detractors, and irrelevant criticism based on Steinbeck's failure to produce another work of comparable stature, Alexander Cowie's judgment, in *The Rise of the American Novel*, that in *The Grapes of Wrath* "most of the new features" in fiction "that have any value find a brilliant and powerful synthesis" [4] has remained the definitive appraisal.

Critics disagree as to which of Hemingway's novels should be called "best," but his most devoted student, Carlos Baker, considers *For Whom the Bell Tolls*, Hemingway's longest and most complex work and the most important literary monument to one of the most portentous events of the thirties, the Spanish Civil War, "a genuinely great novel." [5] Along with Picasso's Guernica mural, Hemingway's novel of Spain in agony, culminating in the description of the Calvary of El Sordo's guerilla band, achieves one of the highest purposes of social fiction as it bares the sufferings of a still largely primitive people that lie behind the headlines, about the destructive capacity of the mechanized force let loose upon these people.

The inclusion of Faulkner's *The Hamlet* in this trio is likely to be most controversial. Almost ignored by reviewers of a period that was just beginning to discover Faulkner, the novel was dismissed for years as simply a collection of related pseudo-folk tales about Southern grotesques. After Peter Lisca and others demonstrated *The Hamlet*'s organic unity, it was viewed principally as a kind of modern myth of man's productive and destructive capacities.[6] Without wishing to deny the mythological implications of Faulkner's extraordinary story, I would also like to argue for a more balanced approach that reveals it, too, as a painstaking and accurate revelation of the Mississippi state of mind that not only reflects much thinking in the modern (and ancient) world, but that has been specifically responsible for many of the continuing tensions and tragedies that have resulted in the United States from the racial situation and the nation's slowness in taking appropriate steps to remedy it.

All the books of Faulkner's Yoknapatawpha saga are

social novels in the sense that they shed psychological light on conspicuous events in recent Southern and general American history: the decline of the Bourbons (*The Sound and the Fury*), the degeneration of the yeoman (*As I Lay Dying*), the growth of native fascism (*Light in August*), the repetition of old errors when the oppressed rise to avenge themselves (*Absalom, Absalom!*). I think, however, that *The Hamlet* is the most important social novel of the group because it deals with the behavior that has had the strongest impact, not just in making Mississippi the most backward and stagnant state in the nation, but also in hindering the progress of the whole country and making the United States appear ridiculous through the presence in Congress of such megalomaniacs as Senator James K. Vardaman, Senator Theodore Bilbo, and Representative John Rankin. *The Hamlet* depicts the exploitation of the ignorant and paranoid "redneck" by utterly amoral persons motivated by a gross lust for personal power.

An examination of the backgrounds of these three novels, I hope to show, aids in understanding the fatal forces at work during the dying era. By focusing upon the political forces reflected in *The Hamlet*, the sociological theorizing culminating in *The Grapes of Wrath*, and the literary isolationism that finds its most dignified artistic embodiment in *For Whom the Bell Tolls*, I hope that it can be demonstrated that the three American writers of the period whom the world has subsequently most highly honored, present—probably quite unintentionally—in books published at the summit of their careers a living monument to some of the most characteristic forces that brought their world to its death throes.

The three novels upon which I concentrate were not, of course, the only social fiction to appear in 1939 and 1940, but the authors whose names had become most strongly identified during the two preceding decades with the social novel contributed disappointingly little during the last months of the dying age. Although Sinclair Lewis had as recently as 1935, in *It Can't Happen Here,* written seriously if somewhat woodenly of the threat of fascism to the United States and had even later worked intermittently on novels about labor leadership and the Negro problem, his contribution to fiction during the critical year in which the long-threatened collapse occurred was *Bethel Merriday,* an affectionate confection about a stage-struck young Connecticut girl who learns to become a trouper. Dorothy Canfield Fisher took over from Lewis the initiative against fascism; but *Seasoned Timber,* which tells of the conflict that ensues in the summer of 1937 when a wealthy trustee wills at least a million dollars to a down-at-the-heels secondary school in Vermont if it will exclude Jews, makes the incipient native fascists such thoroughly repugnant creatures that they are no more impressive than the cardboard figures in shooting galleries.

John Dos Passos' first novel after the completion of the *U. S. A.* trilogy was an enormous disappointment, not because it marked the beginning of the author's retreat to conservatism, but because the main character in *Adventures of a Young Man* never undergoes any change that sustains interest in the episodic recital of his career from his early misadventures as counselor at a boys' camp to his death at the hands of the Loyalist forces he attempts to aid in the Spanish Civil War. The whole story is told in the brief second chapter in which young Glenn Spotswood unprotestingly takes the blame for an act of childish brutality that he had protested but that had been attributed to him by the victim that he had tried to save. Glenn is simply the traditional fall guy, the "patsy" of Tennessee Williams's *Camino Real,* the "sad sack" of World War II cartoon fame. He is, as a ten-year-old pointed out to Thomas Parkinson, what some of the epic heroes of the past were, simply stupid,[7] so that his death at the hands of his supposed friends is not tragic or even pathetic, but inevitable. His goose has been cooked from the day he emerged in print as a lisping babe.

The "strike" novel had flourished during the thirties, but two aspiring writers failed to make significant additions to the genre at the end of the decade. Albert Maltz, recently converted from play-writing to tale-telling, might have provided a chilling and momentous account of the rise of the fascistic, strike-breaking Black Legion in the Midwest in his *The Underground Stream*, but he became so obsessed with trying to provoke sympathy for one martyred Communist organizer that he never allowed his other characters to come to life. Elliott Paul was scarcely a new writer, but *The Stars and Stripes Forever* was his first "social novel" in a decade. Unfortunately Paul, who had been driven back to the United States after long expatriation only by the Spanish Civil War, appeared to tire of his complicated account of a strike before he finished it, so that what might have been a provocative account of the struggle between paternalistic employers and employees concerned about the recognition of their dignity as individuals, ends in a violent apocalypse that leaves the paternalist curdled into fascist "sitting on top of the world." Paul's cynicism is understandable in view of his own crushing experiences on a small Balearic island, but his novel seems the result of personal outrage rather than detached observation. He was probably well-advised in subsequently abandoning the novel and devoting himself to the popular personal reminiscences that had begun with his *Life and Death of a Spanish Town*.

Two writers who had functioned as the social conscience of the early thirties failed to produce even as satisfactory visions of the late thirties as Paul, because of the artificiality and thinness of the books in which they attempted to deal with two of the most distressing manifestations of native American fascism: lynching and anti-Semitism.

Trouble in July was Erskine Caldwell's first novel in four years, most of which he had spent traveling with photographer Margaret Bourke-White collecting material for collaborative essays on rural Southerners and Czechoslovakians. Although lynching was still a serious problem when he wrote (there were seven authenticated lynchings in 1938), the characters in *Trouble in July* are such improbable caricatures that their plight contributes nothing to an understanding of the tense situation in the South. The Negro characters are so kind, guileless, and pure, and the whites so vicious and irrational, that the complexity of the situation disappears in a collection of unconvincing clichés.

In *Tommy Gallgaher's Crusade*, James T. Farrell focused much more sharply on the dangerous effects of anti-Communist and anti-Semitic preaching than Caldwell had on the forces motivating lynchings. Farrell deals with a rabble-rousing Father Moylan, who might as well have been outrightly named Father Coughlin after the enormously successful "radio priest," whose hatred for the New Deal led him to a defense of fascists and warnings against the conspiracies of international Jewry until he was silenced by the outbreak of the war. Farrell's novel characterizes one of the followers that Coughlin attracted as lazy, surly, hostile to his superiors, relieving his frustrations by threatening inoffensive Jews and breaking up small radical rallies. The possibly fifteen-thousand word tract was deservedly praised as a devastatingly accurate portrait of the incipient fascist, but the work was so slender that Tommy's situation was not even completely enough dramatized to make its significance clear to those not already aware of the menace of the rabble rouser. Farrell's book appears to have been written, not like *The Grapes of Wrath*, to enlighten and warn an uncomprehending public, but to capitalize upon the widespread dislike for Coughlin and his ilk by selling what should have been an inexpensive pamphlet as an extravagantly printed book.

Two books by relatively new novelists that shared the 1939 American Booksellers' Awards with *The Grapes of Wrath* were of unusual significance. Chosen as the "most original" work was Dalton Trumbo's harrowing account of a multiple amputee veteran of World War I, *Johnny Got His Gun*, while Elgin Groseclose's account of the persecution of the Armenians in *Ararat* was cited as "the booksellers' discovery." It is unfortunate that neither novel has continued to receive attention, for they are two of the most successful embodiments in American fiction of the warring philosophies of communism and Christianity that have inspired so many high-minded literary disasters. While Trumbo's novel suffers from the incorporation into it of too much unassimilated propaganda, its story remains harrowing, and it provides a more useful contrast with the outstanding social novels of its period than most defective works which suffer from the author's confused thinking and deficient inventiveness. *Ararat* powerfully illustrates, on the other hand, how traditional beliefs may still generate successful fiction. Surely it is curious to find that the two ends of the spectrum of twentieth-century faith found their most powerful dramatic embodiments in the hands of their most successful American exponents during the same brief period of the collapse of the world they sought to redeem; it is even more remarkably curious evidence of the catholicity of American booksellers' taste that such diametrically opposed books shared an award.

The two authors were not to repeat their success: Dalton Trumbo abandoned fiction for motion-picture scriptwriting after one more trivial and contrived story, and Elgin Groseclose withdrew into historical accounts that have scarcely been noticed. The two years under consideration here also marked the high-water point in the careers of the three principal novelists under consideration. Again, there is likely to be little dispute that Steinbeck has

never again equalled *The Grapes of Wrath*; one of
Faulkner's most ambitious undertakings, *A Fable*, lay far
in the future, but few find it the equal of *The Hamlet*,
which brought together some of the best tales that the
author had contrived during the thirties, which also saw
the publication of his most highly praised novels. While
many do consider Hemingway's *The Old Man and the Sea*
one of his outstanding works, it is technically a puny thing
beside the vast and organically sound architecture of *For
Whom the Bell Tolls*. The beginning of the forties marked
the beginning of a decline in the work of our most
distinguished social novelists.

Perhaps the most striking evidence, however, that some
kind of terminal had been reached was that the American
writer whose name had been for three decades most
conspicuously linked with the kind of social novel that he
could fairly be said to have invented decided suddenly in
1939 to abandon his efforts to reform the world and to
retreat into reminiscence.

Only a few years previously Upton Sinclair had run for
governor of California on his E.P.I.C. (End Poverty in
California) platform, and within the immediately preceding years of 1937 and 1938 he had ground out tracts about
current events with his accustomed vigor: *No Pasaran!*, his
contribution to the Spanish Republican cause; *Flivver
King* and *Little Steel*, exposés of the inner corruption of
two of America's most powerful industries. Sensing, however, that an end was coming, Sinclair decided to withdraw
from his characteristically active involvement in affairs and
to look back over the era through which he had lived,
beginning with a story of the machinations culminating in
the first World War. With almost uncanny aptitude, he
chose for the first book of the sequence that was to win
more readers than his crusading novels of the thirties a title
that is a slogan for the period: *World's End*.

Sinclair was to devote the next decade—sitting out the

despicable but predictable catastrophe of World War II—to shaping his legend of Lanny Budd, incredibly handsome and gifted bastard of a munitions king and an international beauty queen, whose charm and vigor won him the right to sit in on the making of history. Although Sinclair chose to fashion his fable, not around a young fighter from the ranks, but rather a fairy-tale prince who fulfilled everyman's dream of being young, dashing, and wealthy, the Lanny Budd books cannot simply be lightly written off as appealing fantasies. Necessarily superficial, they are still spiced with an old campaigner's vigorous ironies about the foibles of the powerful, a generous dose of slyly inserted propaganda for the liberal causes he had long espoused, and venomously apt portraits of the great of the era. There are few pleasanter ways to supplement the reading of the history of the early twentieth century than to follow at the same time the fast-moving adventures of the graceful and impetuously idealistic young American superman through whom Upton Sinclair allows the reader to indulge his desire to play a role in shaping world affairs.

This was a period for such voluminous reminiscence. Posthumously, Thomas Wolfe's vast account of the struggles of the uncompromising individualist appeared in *The Web and the Rock* and *You Can't Go Home Again*. In France, Jules Romains's chronicle of twentieth-century French history reached its climax in *Verdun*, the story of the central struggle in World War I, just in time for the novel to serve as an epitaph for a Paris vanquished at last in World War II. Josephine Herbst was bringing her multivolumed, socially conscious cliff-hanger about the fragmentation of the tight world of an American family to a conclusion in *Rope of Gold*. Few novels, however, capture the recklessly irresponsible flavor of the age with the authenticity of Sinclair's first chronicle of Lanny Budd. The irrepressible veteran hit precisely the right note to tell the story of the Age of Paris. Although the action whirls occasionally to Connecticut, the British countryside, a

German feudal estate, the Côte d'Azur—the real world of the people who mattered in the *belle epoque* early in the century—it centers around Paris, capital of the arts and intrigues of the age; and as befits a people who tried to bring to life their good and wicked dreams without recking consequences, it is a superficially charming and fundamentally sordid fantasy.

Significantly, too, no beginning novelists emerged during 1939 and 1940 to occupy the places that Upton Sinclair and Sinclair Lewis had once held. The proletarian literary movement, one of the most productive sources of new social novelists in the middle thirties, had just about run its course by 1939. A novelist like Pietro di Donato, who brought a fresh and vigorous viewpoint to the American social scene, was a victim of the very irresponsibility that destroyed the age, and even Richard Wright was diverted from developing as an artist. The only beginning social novelist later to exceed his original promise was Robert Penn Warren, an academician, who championed a vastly different approach to the creative arts from his bumptious and often slapdash predecessors in social analysis.

It should finally be noted as of far more than passing curiosity that these same years saw, too, the publication by the world's outstanding experimental writer of his protracted efforts to produce the monumental embodiment of all the new literary techniques that the Age of Paris had fathered. After the long awaited appearance in 1939 of James Joyce's dream history of everybody, *Finnegans Wake*, it was clear that if there was still to be an *avant garde*, it would have to move in a new direction. It is thus fair to say that 1939 and 1940 marked not only the end of an era in social and political history, but the end of a literary generation, especially in the creation of the social novel.

New writers would also need to appear if a new age emerged from the ashes.

IN TREATING Faulkner's *The Hamlet* as a social novel, my intention is not to draw, as John Cullen delightfully does in *Old Times in the Faulkner Country*, explicit parallels between real people and Faulkner's characters. Nor do I intend to construct a picture of Mississippi at the turn of the century from clues in the novel. Rather I wish to confront the historical record of the period with Faulkner's portrayal in the novel of human beings dramatizing their values through their actions. This confrontation shows, I believe, how the "Snopesism" that reached the peak of its power during the decade of the depression arose from the political situation that developed gradually in Mississippi after Reconstruction and reached its climax just after the turn of the century about the time that Flem Snopes began his rise.

To support the validity of this effort, I call upon Faulkner himself, who said during his visit to Japan, "In my country, an artist is nothing. Nobody pays attention to him. . . . In my country, instead of asking the artist what makes children commit suicide, they go to the Chairman of General Motors and ask him. That is true. If you make a million dollars, you know all the answers." [1] But this cynical outburst means that Faulkner did believe that we might ask the artist. He also said during these talks at Nagano that he loved his country enough "to want to cure its faults" by shaming and criticizing it. He felt that the writer "should not be just a 'recorder' of man—he should give man some reason to believe that man can be better than he is." [2] The novelist must thus go beyond "the facts," but this does not mean that he necessarily ignores them. *The Hamlet* certainly reflects archetypal patterns of behavior, but to treat the novel exclusively as a kind of universal myth is to miss some of its vital qualities. Cleanth Brooks observes that more than any other novel of Faulkner's, this first volume of the Snopes saga introduces us to "a strange and special world," [3] but this world is no fantasy. It is the Mississippi of the half century between Reconstruction and the Great Depression.

I remember, as what Faulkner would call a "chap," studying civics in a large Northern city and developing from election returns a concept of Mississippi as monolithically single-minded, a place where the most unswerving kind of conformity was not demanded, but simply taken for granted as the price of existence. I had to go to Mississippi to discover the error in this concept. It is correct, of course, to the extent that "White Supremacy" continues to be almost universally the fundamental tenet of local faith. As very recent events show, those foolhardy enough to challenge this tenet find the defenders of the tradition still willing to turn the state into a bloody battleground.

Mississippians, however, even when embattled, can agree among themselves on little except the divinely ordained inferiority of nonwhites. If the racial issue did not necessitate an uneasy united front, Mississippi would probably be even more politically paralyzed by irreconcilable sectional cleavages than such sites of urban-rural friction as New York and Illinois. The causes of this disunity go far back into the history of the state, little known to outsiders because delving into Mississippi affairs has little appeal for the fastidious.

At the time of the Civil War, the state was just emerging from frontier conditions. Its greatest growth had occurred between 1830 and 1840 when migrants from the Eastern part of the South tripled the 1817 population of 70,000. This was the period during which—as Faulkner describes in the violent pages of *Absalom, Absalom!* and the interchapters of *Requiem for a Nun*—plantations and communities were violently wrested from the virgin soil. By 1860, too, the state boasted some of the wealthiest citizens of the nation.

The Civil War prostrated the state; many of the able-bodied men who had directed its growth were dead or discredited. With the abolition of slavery, the plantation system needed a vast reorganization, for which the state had neither the money, the energy, nor the objective intelligence. Away from the regions along the Mississippi and Yazoo Rivers, the thin, exploited soil was already showing signs of exhaustion.

Mention of the soil brings us to the outstandingly important fact that Mississippi is divided into three quite varying sections. Most of the power in the early days of the state centered in the rich Delta, lying between and along the Mississippi and the Yazoo. Here were located the ante bellum plantations that have assumed mythical dimensions as a result of such latter-day extravaganzas as the Natchez pilgrimage. The Delta had early assumed control of state politics and would ever be reluctant to relinquish it.

In another world from the prosperous, flood-prone Delta is the so-called Piney Woods region of Southern Mississippi, a sparsely settled lumbering area with poor soil, whose principal products have been the lumbering brutes who have given the University of Mississippi winning football teams and Senator Theodore Bilbo. Most of the poverty-stricken population of the Piney Woods region is white; the Negroes are largely concentrated in the Delta.

East of the Delta, north of the Piney Woods, rise the "red clay hills," on the western edge of which is Oxford, long Faulkner's home and model for the Jefferson of his Yoknapatawpha saga. This land of "rednecks" combines the worst features of the other two sections: the pretentiousness and aristocratic arrogance of the Delta (there is even a Natchez-like pilgrimage in Holly Springs, thirty miles north of Oxford) with the poverty, exhausted soil, and bigotry of the Piney Woods. This combination is immortally captured in that scene in *The Hamlet* in which Ab Snopes grinds horse dung into Major de Spain's hundred-dollar French rug (p. 17).[4] Clearly this ill-favored region, which has fewer Negroes than the Delta, but more than the Piney Woods, holds the balance of power between the fastness of the Bourbon traditionalists and the marches of the illiterate barbarians.

After Mississippi regained its statehood in 1870, a power struggle began. The radical Republican machine managed to force Negro rule on Mississippi longer than on most of the South, but it was at last supplanted in 1876, largely through the diplomatic manipulations of Lucius Quintus Cincinatus Lamar, a man dedicated to his own advancement, who shrewdly succeeded in inserting himself into the confidence of even suspicious Northerners. Lamar provided almost the only powerful link between the Old and the New Mississippi. Born in 1825 in Georgia (from which many influential Mississippians had migrated), he had even served in the legislature of his home state before moving with his father-in-law, Augustus Baldwin Longstreet, distinguished jurist and author of *Georgia Scenes*, who had become chancellor of the newly established University of Mississippi.

Lamar soon projected himself with enthusiasm into the affairs of his adopted home and distinguished himself as the author of its secession ordinance. Soon proving physically unable to endure combat, he became the Confederate emissary to Imperial Russia. After the war he returned to teach law at the University of Mississippi, from which strategic spot on the boundary between hills and Delta, he exercised such remarkable powers of political manipulation that he became the first Democrat elected to the state legislature since the end of the War, in the very year (1872) that the Amnesty Act restored full political privileges to disfranchised Southerners.

Subsequently, he became the first white United States Senator from Mississippi since the hostilities, and he capped his career by achieving the greatest national distinctions for which a former rebel could have hoped—a place first in Cleveland's cabinet as Secretary of the Interior and at last an appointment as associate justice of the Supreme Court. Albert D. Kirwan says with unquestionable accuracy that at the time White rule was restored in Mississippi, Lamar's "approval was almost sufficient to guarantee election—his disapproval, to insure defeat." [5] Precisely thirty-five years later, in 1911, James Kimble Vardaman was in the same position; but he was by no stretch of the imagination Lamar's heir. Indeed "The Great White Chief," as Vardaman was fondly known, consolidated his power by crushing at last the spokesman of the postwar "Bourbon" party that Lamar founded. The story of Mississippi politics in the year that Faulkner's *The Hamlet* illuminates is the story of the shift of power from Lamar to Vardaman, as the story of the novel is that of the shift of power from Will Varner to Flem Snopes.

To understand what happened, we must first realize that the late nineteenth-century Bourbons in Mississippi were not identical with the aristocratic, flamboyant Bourbon planters who controlled the state before the Civil War. As Kirwan points out in *Revolt of the Rednecks*, those who stubbornly held to the past and refused to pay lip service to the war amendments "were few in Mississippi politics and they exercised little influence" (p. 8). The new Bourbons were not unsophisticated planters obsessed by dreams like

Thomas Sutpen's of establishing baronial fiefdoms, but, like Lamar, principally corporation lawyers who identified themselves with the aggressive railroads that were responsible for what small economic progress the state made before the end of the century. They inherited the Bourbon name, however, because like their predecessors they fancied themselves the stable and responsible element in the state, in opposition to the poor, dirty, and largely illiterate hill farmers who were beginning to cry for relief.

Agricultural reforms were hard to achieve in Mississippi because the Bourbons equated any effort to break with the Democratic party that they controlled, with a threat to continued white dominance in the state. The black menace was used to hold dissidents in line while ignoring their complaints. It was argued that only complete Democratic unity could prevent a resurgence of Black Republicanism; nor did these selfless leaders rely only on argument to protect the "rednecks" from potential folly. Every device for stuffing ballot-boxes and fixing returns was employed, and not only Negroes were lynched. In a notorious episode in Kemper County in 1877, Judge W. W. Chisholm, a white independent who had been a Republican, two of his teen-aged children, and a British friend were shot as they fled from a jail that a mob had set on fire.[6] Control of the state was almost completely in the hands of the Executive Committee of the Democratic Convention, which was in turn managed by Lamar and his fellow Senator, the corporation lawyer James Z. George, who was apparently responsible for the provisions in the Mississippi Constitution of 1890 that at last "solved" the problem of formally disfranchising the Negro—the poll-tax and the "understanding" of the State Constitution clauses. Cleanth Brooks notes that "the Negro has hardly any part" in Faulkner's *The Hamlet*, and indeed, during this period, Negroes played no effective role in the political life of the state.

The new constitution, which did cut the actual vote in

the state nearly in half, served, however, only to further dissension among the whites. By 1890 it had become apparent, for one thing, that the Delta, while monopolizing political power, was not paying anything like its proportionate share of state taxes. The campaign of 1891 between incumbent Senator George and Ethelbert Barksdale, representative of the insurgent farmers, for electors was one of the bitterest and most violent in the state's history.

The defeat of the farmers is generally attributed to Bourbon control of the party machinery, but it is doubtful that affairs in Mississippi can be thus rationally explained. Another element that played an enormous part is explained in Kirwan's summary of the campaign in 1892 between the Bourbon candidates for Congress and the Populists, to whom the farmers had turned:

> [The Populists] charged that "the Bourbon Democrats" had foisted [the franchise provisions of the Constitution] on the people in an attempt to curtail the privilege of voting.
>
> The Democrats answered the challenge with the old rallying cry of white supremacy. They accused the Populists of favoring Negro suffrage . . . .
>
> To all the clamor which the Populists made for reform, the Democrats answered that there were some things more important than reforms in the economy. A Populist victory, they warned, would result in Negro supremacy and the degradation of Southern womanhood. (*Revolt of the Rednecks*, p. 95)

The "things" that mattered more than reform were, of course, those elements of the "Mississippi tradition" of which the Bourbons considered themselves the sole defenders; as long as they could convince the voters to accept the Bourbon candidates as the defenders of whites against blacks, the reform candidates could never win by insisting upon debating economic issues on their own merits. *The Hamlet* suggests through the portrayal of characters like

Henry Armstid and Mink Snopes and WallStreet Panic Snopes that many of Mississippi's "peasants" were paranoid; here art follows reality.

As if to test the hypothesis that the farmer's party could achieve victory only when it found a spokesman who could beat the Bourbons at their own game by outshouting them, James K. Vardaman appeared on the scene.

Vardaman has lent his name to two of Faulkner's most repulsive characters—the feeble-minded youngest Bundren child in *As I Lay Dying*, and one of the loathesome Snopes twins who try to agitate the man who may be their grandfather into a stroke in *The Town*. Although Vardaman died in 1930, he still lingers in our commercial folklore as the prototype for Al Capp's Senator Phogbound and other mass-media solons. He injected new drama into political campaigning by appearing in Mississippi's numerous hamlets in an eight-wheeled lumber cart drawn by several pairs of white oxen, dressed all in white, with his dark hair falling down to his shoulders, and demanding that the dangerous practice of educating Negroes cease.

He was of the post-Civil War generation, having been born in 1861 to parents who had migrated from Mississippi to Texas, but who returned home after the conflict. He grew up and attended public schools—like the one I. O. Snopes conducts in *The Hamlet*—in Yalobusha County, directly below Lafayette County, where Faulkner lived, and only a few miles from the Frenchman's Bend country. When only twenty-one, Vardaman qualified for the bar and set up practice in Winona, a seedy county seat, strategically located on the road between Memphis and Jackson that forms the boundary between the Delta and the hills.

Soon he was editing the community newspaper, and in 1890—just as Flem Snopes progressed from the hamlet to Jefferson—Vardaman moved into the Delta to the flourishing city of Greenwood, which he soon began to represent in the state legislature. In 1895 he turned up as a candidate for governor, but withdrew for obscure reasons a month before the nominating convention. Since he had returned from the Spanish-American War a hero, however, he was less easy to deal with in 1899, when the last election was held in which the state convention nominated the candidate for governor. When he saw, however, during the first night's balloting that he could not muster the needed strength, he, along with other contenders, withdrew in favor of the incumbent's candidate.

The situation changed vastly, however, when by political maneuverings that are still not clear, a law was passed over Delta opposition providing for a statewide party primary to replace the scandal-ridden conventions. Vardaman was one of the two candidates to achieve the largest number of votes in the first primary; in the run-off, the newspapers observed that the fight was between "the conservative business element of the state," represented by an old Confederate soldier, and the upstart Vardaman (*Revolt of the Rednecks*, p. 159). But instead of arguing "issues," as his predecessors had when seeking vainly to unseat the Bourbons, Vardaman went to the people with dramatic speeches on the racial issue, arguing against education for Negroes and calling for repeal of the Fourteenth and Fifteenth amendments to the federal Constitution. Even the opposition agreed that Vardaman owed his victory to the revival of the white supremacy question and the new primary law which allowed him to exercise his magnetism directly on the kind of backwoods audience that buys the spotted horses in *The Hamlet*.

Vardaman's greatest tests came, however, during his campaigns for the Senate. Senators were still elected indirectly, but in Mississippi the candidates had since 1890 been nominated in the party primary. Vardaman made his first attempt at a senate seat in 1908 when he opposed incumbent John Sharp Williams in a campaign that featured—particularly as the principal issue in the only face-to-face debate between the contenders at Meridian on July 4, 1907—Vardaman's proposal for repealing the Constitutional amendments. So close was the election that Williams, the Delta planter, despite his organizational support, won by only 648 votes. Even while hailing the victory, the Bourbon press saw trouble coming.

It was not long arriving. The Bourbons had been able to hold on by the narrow margin that they did only because they had been able to maintain the illusion that they were the friends of all whites against the blacks. At Christmas, 1909, Mississippi's other senator died suddenly. Since the primary to replace him would not be held until 1911, the legislature had a free hand in naming his successor. As Kirwan says, "a contest was precipitated which was to have tremendous consequences on the politics of the state" (p. 191). Vardaman was pitted against Leroy Percy, a Delta planter and graduate of the University of the South at Sewanee, Tennessee. No more perfect candidate to maintain Bourbon tradition could have been found. Percy's son, William Alexander Percy, was later to produce, in *Lanterns on the Levee*, the book that articulates the Bourbon philosophy. Certainly Percy specified in this book the real issue in his father's campaigns against Vardaman, when he described the opponent as "a kindly, vain demagogue unable to think," who "looked like a top-notch medicine man" and stood for all that the elder Percy considered "vulgar and dangerous." [7] What none of the Bourbons would have said publicly during the campaigns, young Percy also admits in his book when he describes the poor whites to whom Vardaman appealed as "intellectually and spiritually . . . inferior to Negroes, whom they hate." He also describes them as a "gang of poor degenerates" that "lynch Negroes, that mistake hoodlumism for wit, and cunning for intelligence, that attend revivals and fight and fornicate in the bushes afterwards." [8] Vardaman's party believed that the Bourbons harbored such feelings, but the problem was to trap these canny politicians into expressing them so that they would be discredited in the eyes of those whose votes they sought.

There was no opportunity for a showdown during the legislative election, since the caucusing was secret. On the first ballot Vardaman led with 71 out of 170 votes; but he was finally defeated by Percy, after all other candidates had been forced out, six weeks later on the fifty-eighth ballot by 87 votes to 82. The caucus was marked by every conceivable illicit effort to influence votes, and its aftermath nearly led to the expulsion of Theodore Bilbo from the state legislature for his ambiguous role in some vote buying.

The voting ended in February, 1910. Although the next primary, for the full Senate term, would not be held for nearly two years (in November, 1911), campaigning between the same two men started almost at once. This time Vardaman could make his sensational appeals directly to the electorate, and Percy relied, as usual, on a counterappeal to people's conservatism. But the contest was tense and, as the title of subsection of *The Hamlet* points out, summers in Mississippi are long and hot. Tempers were already frayed by the long wrangle during the secret caucus. Violence sprang up again, centering around Bilbo, who was beaten into insensibility with a pistol by a man whom Bilbo had said was "a cross between a mongrel and a cur, conceived in a nigger graveyard at midnight, suckled by a sow, and educated by a fool." [9] Such episodes, however, served only to build up sympathy for the group that cast itself in the underdog role. The catastrophe for the Bourbons, for which W. A. Percy has provided the apt title "Sideshow Götterdämmerung," occurred on July 4, 1910.

As in previous elections, the candidates generally avoided confronting each other; but at Lauderdale Spring, near Meridian, on the holiday that always brought out the greatest crowds for political speechmaking, Percy was tricked into sharing the platform with Vardaman's lieutenant, Bilbo. Percy had promised his supporters to avoid personal attacks, but after listening to Bilbo, he lost control of himself and denounced both Vardaman and his ally. Kirwan reports in *Revolt of the Rednecks* that Percy said in part:

> It was not unusual for people to assemble, "out of idle curiosity," to view an unusual dwarf, a three-legged man, or a two-headed calf. Such exhibitions of physical monstrosities had no elevating effect; but the "exhibition of a moral monstrosity," such as was made in the person of Bilbo that day, "has a debasing and degrading effect." (p. 221)

The Bourbon press hailed the speech and reprinted it, but later had cause to regret this premature elation. All through Percy's diatribe, Bilbo had sat on a porch in a manner remarkably like Flem Snopes's, smiling quietly and listening, as Snopes did to old Will Varner.

But the greatest damage was done that same day at another flyspeck, Godbold Wells, where heckled by another crowd of bumpkins, Percy completely lost control and called his auditors "cattle" and "rednecks." These remarks turned the tide. As Kirwan reports, they "were adopted by the Vardaman following, and wherever Vardaman went to speak he was greeted by crowds of men wearing red neckties and was carried in wagons drawn by oxen" (p. 212). In the largest vote cast in Mississippi up to that time, Vardaman won a clear victory in the first primary with 76,000 votes to his opponents' combined 50,000. While many forces unquestionably influenced this surprising vote, the influence of Percy's ill-advised and widely circulated attacks upon "rednecks" is incalculable. The contempt of the Delta planter for "white trash" had been forced out into the open at last.

What must be observed with the same kind of horror that Faulkner's *The Hamlet* inspires, is that even this hurried account of thirty-five ugly years in Mississippi politics shows the lack of influence of significant economic and social issues in determining elections and the vast importance of irrational appeals to fears and prejudices, especially to the continuing fear of black domination at the time when the completely subjugated Negro posed little threat. How could the whole political history of a state hinge so much on irrationality and the opportunistic exploiting of it? History provides the record of what happened; but when we seek to understand the motives behind the events, we must turn to the intuitions of the perceptive novelist.

ii

Despite extensive commentaries on Faulkner's Snopes novels, I cannot find that anyone has previously called attention to the way in which the geography of Frenchman's Bend, the community that gives *The Hamlet* its title, reproduces in miniature the physiological characteristics of the state of Mississippi. In the first paragraph of the novel, the setting is described as "a section of rich river-bottom country . . . hill-cradled and remote," and in the fantastic tale told of an idiot's romance with a cow, we find a fuller description of the relationship between valley and hill.

> A mile back he had left the rich, broad, flat river-bottom country and entered the hills—a region which topographically was the final blue and dying echo of the Appalachian mountains. . . . Now it was a region of scrubby second-growth pine and oak among which dogwood bloomed until it too was cut to make cotton spindles, and old fields where not even a trace of furrow showed any more, gutted and gullied by forty years of rain and frost and heat into plateaus choked with rank sedge and briers loved of rabbits and quail coveys, and crumbling ravines striated red and white with alternate sand and clay. (p. 196)

The story is thus set against the background of an area that harbors the same tensions as exist on a larger scale between the Delta and hills of the state.

Originally the hamlet was the site of the Old Frenchman's Place, "a tremendous pre-Civil War plantation." Much of the character of the people of the region is established by Faulkner's description of the reaction of three successive waves of settlers to this landmark.

Its builder had "quite possibly been a foreigner, though not necessarily French," but "all that remained of him was the river bed which his slaves had straightened for almost ten miles to keep his land from flooding." "Even his name was forgotten," Faulkner continues, "his pride but a legend about the land he had wrested from the jungle and tamed as a monument to that appellation which those who came after him . . . could not even read, let alone pronounce, and which now had nothing to do with any once-living man at all" (p. 4). The Old Frenchman thus typifies that generation which built Mississippi but vanished almost without record, leaving only a myth behind to be fleshed out as pilgrimage directors people the past or as Faulkner's Quentin Compson and his Canadian roommate at Harvard reconstruct the tale of Thomas Sutpen in *Absalom, Absalom!* But though he has become a myth, the old Frenchman still exerts, like the prewar Bourbons, a tangible influence on later generations through "the stubborn tale of money he buried somewhere about the place" (p. 4).

At the time the novel begins the plantation that the phantasmal old Frenchman wrested from the wilderness is a ruin in the receivership of Will Varner, as all of old Mississippi is a wasteland at the disposal of railroad builders. Varner is perhaps the most difficult character in the novel for the non-Mississippian to understand, for he seems as avaricious and amoral as the Snopeses; yet the author's sentiments about him are clearly ambiguous. This ambiguity is caught in a description that Faulkner attributes to Judge Benbow, one of Jefferson's patricians, "a milder-mannered man never bled a mule or stuffed a ballot box" (p. 5). Varner not only exploits Frenchman's Bend himself, but he exposes the hamlet and subsequently the whole county to the depredations of the Snopeses in an effort to protect his own holdings. Learning of the Snopeses' reputations as barn-burners, Varner acts first out of prudence and fear, as the postwar Bourbons did to prevent further havoc in an already prostrate state. Later, however, he tolerates Flem beyond the demands of prudence, conniving with him (as the Bourbons did at first with Vardaman) and even calling upon him to save daughter Eula's reputation. Yet despite this trafficking with evil, Varner is never denounced.

Through his treatment of Varner, Faulkner shows his own hand; for he must have felt—as L. Q. C. Lamar did—that there was little that one could do but compromise with evil if Mississippi was not to revert to wilderness. Varner occupied the same position with relationship to his tiny suzerainty that Lamar did to the state. Varner was "the fountainhead if not of law at least of advice and suggestion to a countryside which would have repudiated the term constituency if they had ever heard it. . . . He was a farmer, a usurer, a veterinarian" (p. 5). He owns most of the land in the region, although he is not essentially a planter, but a merchant, investor, and even inventor, who tries to keep the stagnant community alive. Lamar had been obliged to resort to fraud and demagoguery to restore Democratic control in Mississippi; but the region might have been in even worse condition without his efforts. Historians like Kirwan may justly be critical of Lamar's saving the region for obviously selfish reasons, and a modern novelist like Pat Frank can write Mississippi off in *Mister Adam* as an expendable site for nuclear tests, but William Faulkner couldn't—at least not back in the thirties when he was fashioning the early chapters in the

Snopes saga. Behind the books written during the period of his greatest literary activity lies a love of his native soil as passionate and irrational as that the narrator expresses at the end of Gogol's *Dead Souls*.

Will Varner from the viewpoint of one who cares about Mississippi has one powerful redeeming virtue. His efforts, like those of Lamar and his generation, are guided by a desire for the success that eluded the Frenchman and the older Mississippi, rather than for the glory that they sought. Varner tells another character, as he sits "against his background of fallen baronial splendor" in his flour-barrel seat, that he's "trying to find out what it must have felt like to be the fool that would need all this . . . just to eat and sleep in" (p. 7). The Varner who makes this statement is a tragic figure, for just as he is bewildered by the past, he is perplexed by the future. Of his many children, only two—a bellicose coward and a sensual animal—remain at home. He is trying to maintain some human order in a region where generally only those with less than normal human drives remain.

Small wonder, then, that he is willing to close his eyes to the inhuman qualities of Flem Snopes, who, as William Faulkner's brother John has said, is representative of a group which by usurping power made the old residents "aware for the first time of the value of human endeavour." [10] Snopes is, however, as both a fantastic vision of his besting the devil and his impotency suggest, not really human. He sees the ruined old Frenchman's place not as the source of wonder it is to Will Varner, but simply as something to be exploited in his drive for success. Flem belongs to the same breed as Vardaman and his creature Bilbo. Faulkner, who had good reason to hate Bilbo for ousting Murray Faulkner, William's father, from his post as Comptroller of the University of Mississippi during a vendetta against the state system of higher education in 1930, surely felt that Snopesism was monstrous and that

Frenchman's Bend had fallen into the hands of worse than fiends, who made their fortunes by preying upon the ignorance and passions of the "peasants" for whom he names the last section of *The Hamlet*, just as Vardaman and Bilbo preyed upon them in campaigns designed to inflame "White Supremist" sentiments.

The comparison between Snopesism and Vardamanism is most manifest, however, in the portrayal of the conflict that really serves to link together the superficially only casually related episodes of *The Hamlet*—Flem Snopes's effort to complete the subjugation of his environment by overcoming Ratliff, an itinerant sewing-machine salesman.

Ratliff is something far more than a detached observer who gets drawn into the affairs of Frenchman's Bend. The crucial statement about this apostle of modest progress occurs immediately before a conversation that he has with Will Varner about the gift of the Old Frenchman's place to Flem Snopes in return for Flem's marrying Varner's pregnant daughter Eula.

> [Varner] sat the old horse and looked down at Ratliff, the little hard eyes beneath their busy rust-colored brows glinting at the man who was a good deal nearer his son in spirit and intellect and physical appearance too than any of his own get. (p. 180)

Faulkner thus conceives of Ratliff as Varner's true heir; and if the region has any intellectual and spiritual future at all, it depends not upon Varner's apathetic and trouble-making children, but on Ratliff, who has stayed on in Mississippi, even though he, like Will Varner, has abilities that should assure his success elsewhere.

Through this intimation of the relationship between the two men, Faulkner suggests that the expedients to which the men of Lamar's generation yielded were dictated by their hopes for the future. Certainly if Flem Snopes is able to defeat Ratliff, the victim will not be just one man or one small community, but a way of life that some have struggled for generations to preserve.

This struggle that dominates the book first comes into focus when Ratliff, discussing Varner's son Jody's efforts to cope with the Snopeses, comments, "there aint but two men I know can risk fooling with them folks. And just one of them is named Varner, and his front name aint Jody." When Varner asks who the other is, Ratliff replies "pleasantly," "That aint been proved yet neither" (p. 31).

Shortly afterwards, Ratliff first "risks fooling" with the Snopeses by attempting to outwit Flem in a deal involving some apparently worthless goats. Ratliff does best Snopes to the extent of making Flem see "what it feels like" to burn up money, but he loses his profit on the transaction because he has not been cautious enough to discover before getting too deeply involved that Flem has no compunction about exploiting a feeble-minded relative. Whereas Ratliff would use his strength to protect society from being debased by the idiot, Flem will use his to exploit the idiot in victimizing society. This incident supports John Faulkner's attribution of his brother's hatred of Snopeses to their cruel treatment of the epileptic son of an old Oxford family.[11]

The incident also serves to draw the line between Ratliff and Snopes on the basis of their differing concepts of social responsibility and to establish also Ratliff's fatal weakness for acting too precipitately—perhaps even quixotically when his emotions are aroused. This shortcoming is noted by the compassionless Flem, who will be motivated in the future to triumph over this man who has bettered him. After the episode, Ratliff simply sends back to Varner the cryptic message, "It aint been proved yet neither" (p. 101).

The next round is Ratliff's. While Flem is off in Texas waiting for Eula's baby to grow enough to bring back to the hamlet, Ratliff uses his strength—as the Bourbon party did in the secret caucus—to frustrate Lancelot Snopes's vicious scheme to profit from alerting the hamlet's idly curious when his feeble-minded cousin is about to make love to a cow. Certainly by sending Vardaman to Washington, Mississippi provided the curious of the nation with a similarly edifying spectacle.

The next brush with Flem himself, however, produces more equivocal results. The episode of the sale of the spotted horses from Texas remarkably parallels the controversy about vote-buying during the secret caucus for the Mississippi senatorial nomination, since Flem Snopes (like Vardaman) never shows his hand directly, but allows his subalterns to bear the brunt of the ensuing litigation as Vardaman had Bilbo. Ratliff manages to preserve his honor, since he is not duped into buying one of the worthless monsters, but he is embarrassed—as the Bourbons were by counter-revelations during the lurid Bilbo trial—by being obliged to jump from his hotel window when one of the horses gets as far as his door, and he is obliged to see his friends suffer, while further incurring the wrath of the Snopeses for avoiding their trap, just as Percy roused Vardaman's enmity by failing to yield to a mandate of the people. Snopes, after all, by providing the "peasants" with an opportunity to buy the worthless horses, gave the public what it wanted.

Discussing the episode of the horse sale, Ratliff most fully articulates just what the struggle with the Snopeses means to him. Asked if he has returned to the pathetic Henry Armstid the money which his wife had earned weaving at night, Ratliff answers that he could have, but didn't, just as he had not, after the goat episode, burned a promissory note out of merely sentimental concern for a feeble-minded Snopes.

"I wasn't protecting a Snopes from Snopeses; I wasn't even protecting a people from a Snopes. I was protecting something that wasn't even a people, that wasn't nothing but something that dont want nothing but to walk and feel the sun and wouldn't know how to hurt no man even if it would and wouldn't want to even if it could, just like I wouldn't stand by and see you steal a meat-bone from a dog. I never made them Snopeses and I never made the folks that cant wait to bare their backsides to them. I could do more, but I wont. I wont, I tell you!" (p. 367)

Ratliff has no wish to be his brother's keeper. He is a sharp man in a business transaction. As he points out when he deprives the feeble-minded Snopes of the cow for which he has developed an infatuation, he acts because he is "stronger," not "righter" or "any better, maybe" (p. 227). What Ratliff wishes to maintain is an atmosphere in which decency can exist, as it surely cannot in a place where men watch quietly as another beats his wife, "their faces lowered as though brooding upon the earth at their feet" (p. 337), an atmosphere in which one can act spontaneously in behalf of what he believes in. The Snopeses prevent the maintenance of such an atmosphere, for a Flem, who can without showing any emotion at all quietly watch the man beat his wife, is constantly scheming to take advantage of any action by the remaining individuals who are not either cowed into abject submission or motivated by unfeeling calculation. Ratliff is especially angry that efforts to resist the Snopeses are especially handicapped by those so willing to "bare their backsides" to them that they will, like Mrs. Armstid after being victimized by the Snopeses, call Flem "right kind" when he buys her off with a nickel bag of candy, the same kind of "little sweetening for the chaps" (p. 362) that Vardaman and Bilbo so often handed out to the adoring throngs.

In their last contest, Flem Snopes is able to defeat even Ratliff. The whole transaction involving the sale of the old Frenchman's Place is remarkably similar to the Percy–Vardaman campaign of 1910. In this episode, Flem Snopes manages—without saying a word—to persuade Ratliff and some cohorts that there is indeed—as has long been rumored—money buried on the ruined estate, by salting the ruins with a bag of coins. Ratliff then offers to trade

Flem an interest in a lunch counter in Jefferson for the worthless property, so that Flem is last seen riding toward his next conquest, while Ratliff is left quite literally holding the bag.

Flem is able to trick Ratliff for two reasons that have important psychological implications. First, Ratliff, loyal to his native soil, has never been able to give up a baseless illusion that the ruins, which symbolize the mythical ante bellum land of wealth, still hold a buried fortune. His feelings reflect the persisting notion that there was still something for the present in the glamorous past that also led the Bourbon party in Mississippi, beset by upstarts, to turn to Leroy Percy, a candidate representative of traditional departed glories.

Ratliff, furthermore, would not have been victimized if he had not, because of his uncontrollable enthusiasm, failed to open at least one bag of the coins that he and his fellow excavators found. If he had, he would have discovered that the coins were minted after the Civil War and had to have been planted since the old Frenchman had vanished. Flem Snopes had found at last a way to exploit Ratliff's all too human weakness for acting in a moment of passionate enthusiasm without calculating all possible consequences. This is precisely what Bilbo did on July 4, 1910, when he succeeded in baiting Leroy Percy into his intemperate attack on "rednecks." A single slip sent Snopes riding toward Jefferson, Vardaman toward Washington.

Because of his sympathy for the defeated in this episode, Faulkner suggests that spontaneous outbursts of feeling must not be inhibited if man is not to be reduced to an unfeeling automaton. The vice of Snopesism is that its practitioners ape human traits without being fully human. They give man no reason to believe that he can be better than he is; rather they seek to destroy his distinguishing traits of compassion and spontaneity by exploiting them.

As Warren Beck writes in *Man in Motion*, a study of the Snopes trilogy, "Flem is, even more than Popeye [the grotesque criminal in *Sanctuary*], the modern automaton bred by materialism out of original crudeness." [12] The automatism of Faulkner's characters results not, however, from the dehumanizing forces of mechanization that many critics have decried, but from the peculiar political atmosphere in a state in which any true assertion of one's feelings might ruin one's prospects. Certainly the life in Frenchman's Bend is as primitive and unmechanized as life in an organized culture can be. Faulkner's novel sardonically points out that man cannot regain his spontaneity simply by fleeing the city and the machine.

Leadership in Mississippi had become by the early years of the twentieth century, not a matter of positive action to improve conditions, but a negative process of waiting for one's opponent to make a misstep or misstatement that one could pounce upon. Although Faulkner dealt with the period when the Vardamans and Snopeses first gained their power, the same situation prevailed in Mississippi in the 1930's. In fact, the state had slipped back into the hands of the Bilbo–Snopeses after seeming to have escaped from them in the twenties when a falling-out between Bilbo and Governor Lee Russell, a former henchman, restored the Bourbons to power. Bilbo, however, was able to sweep back into the governorship in 1927 in a campaign during which he literally threw bricks. This time he was determined to get control of higher education by moving the University of Mississippi, stronghold of Bourbonism, from remote Oxford to Jackson, where the governor could keep a close eye on it. Although by manipulating appointments to the State Board of Regents, he was able to precipitate a national scandal by firing the Chancellor of the University, forty-five faculty members, and a number of the administrative staff,[13] he was not successful in getting the University moved; and both his personal and professional reputation suffered badly. The depression found him in dire straits; he lost the "dream house" he was building, and by 1934 he was reduced to begging his Bourbon opponent, Senator Pat Harrison, for a humiliating post in the federal bureaucracy, until he had a chance to launch a campaign for a United States Senate seat in 1934.

A. Wigfall Green, Bilbo's scholarly biographer, who has long been intimately familiar with Mississippi politics, thinks that a "vibrant and colorful and popular" opponent in the 1934 Senate race would have "drawn and quartered Bilbo politically," [14] but the Bourbon mind seems never to learn. Against Bilbo, the traditionalists pitted Hubert Stephens, who as Green points out had already offended the "rednecks" by saying that "from the fetid filth of Mississippi politics as it exists today, offensive odors and tempests of disgrace have swept into every portion of the nation." [15] The Bourbons lost, and Bilbo regained the power that he was to wield until fatal illness and shrewder opposition caught up with him after World War II. Faulkner's *The Hamlet* presents, however, a precisely accurate portrait of the kind of figure that stood before the world—quite conspicuously in view of Bilbo's penchant for filibustering and making insulting statements—as a symbol of Mississippi at the end of the thirties.

Small wonder that a state whose ignorant prejudices made it putty in the hands of sharp and unscrupulous individuals motivated by a desire for self-aggrandizement often resembled an armed camp and that many of its able young people, like most of the children of Varner and of the owner of the barn in which the idiot hid his cow, left home and sometimes simply vanished. Certainly the atmosphere of constraint, not unique to Mississippi but fostered there by the unusual poverty, the fear of violence, and the threat of Negro resurgence, left the state almost completely in the hands of the kind of apathetic characters that gather around Varner's store in *The Hamlet*, the completely irrational and potentially psychotic buyers of spotted horses, and those greedy and cynical enough to observe this scene without revulsion and to attempt to advance themselves by callously exploiting the apathetic and the irrational.

Faulkner himself commented on this callous exploitation characteristic of the Snopeses, when he told an undergraduate audience at the University of Virginia that Flem "had to teach himself a certain shrewdness about people in order to make the money which he believed was the end of existence. . . . He probably understood all of his life [all] that he ever needed to understand." [16]

Surely the same thing could be said of Vardaman and Bilbo. It is hard to believe that it is purely coincidental that Faulkner began to publish the tales that were subsequently incorporated into *The Hamlet* at the very time that his family was most directly affected by Bilboism through the vengeful dismissal from the University of Mississippi of those officials that had dared stand in the path of the power hungry.

Thus while *The Hamlet* is not a story of Mississippi politics, it is a revelation of the inner workings of the culture that produced the politics. It gives the sensitive reader evidence that allows him to "Think Mississippian." Perhaps this is a dubious distinction, but it is one that can provide a vital perspective on some of the spasms that have for decades flowed over state boundaries to wrack our whole culture.

3 A TROUBLED NATION –
"HOW NICE IT'S GONNA BE, MAYBE, IN CALIFORNIA"

DURING THE TWENTIES AND THIRTIES, large numbers of owners of small farms in the Southern and Southwestern states, as a result of the exhaustion of their soil and the continued depression of farm prices, lost their land to mortgage holders and became tenants or "share croppers." When the prolonged drought and accompanying severe dust storms of the 1930's resulted in the loss of a succession of crops, even the tenant farming system no longer worked and, in order to protect investments, the holding companies evicted the croppers and threw many small farms together into large ones that could be efficiently operated.

Instead of staying home and demanding some form of local relief, many evicted tenants took to the road like modern gypsies and toured the agricultural states in search of seasonal work. They were especially attracted to fertile and prosperous California. At first the large-scale West Coast farmers and canners encouraged the migration in order to assure themselves a supply of cheap and easily managed labor during the brief harvest seasons. Drought, evictions, and migration continued, however, longer than shortsighted manipulators had speculated, and in the late thirties the migration into California was getting out of control. Panicked, the Californians responded by enforcing an anti-migrant law which provided penalties for bringing the destitute into the state and by employing repressive police measures to control restlessness and labor agitation. This frightening and potentially explosive situation was eased only in the early 1940's when the increasing tempo of defense preparations provided an insatiable market for both agricultural and inexperienced factory labor.

All but the last chapter in this depressing history John Steinbeck illustrates in *The Grapes of Wrath*, through both the story of the migrant Joad family and the symbolic and polemical "inter-chapters" that depict the general situation and bring out the universal implications of the Joad story as it specifically illustrates aspects of the agricultural depression. Although the novel was attacked by many offended at the picture Steinbeck drew and though small inaccuracies can be found in the work—which is a novel and not a textbook—*The Grapes of Wrath* can be read, among other things, as a chillingly graphic portrayal of some shocking events of the thirties.

To treat the novel, however, as simply social history is to miss its significance. One seeking information about the period is better advised to turn to Steinbeck's "Their Blood is Strong," a collection of reports about conditions that he wrote for the *San Francisco News* as a result of firsthand observations of the migrant camps, and to the detailed and complementary studies by Carey McWilliams, then California Commissioner of Immigration and Housing, *Factories in the Fields* and *Ill Fares the Land*. I have already collected materials from these sources and others that describe events in the Dust Bowl and California during the thirties in *A Companion to "The Grapes of Wrath*," and it would be idle to repeat this factual background of the novel. I am interested in this study in the novel not as a mirror—however accurate—but as a creative vision that helps us to understand how the events it depicts came about.

Steinbeck's novel has actually been more frequently attacked as art than as propaganda. It has been charged that it lacks artistic unity and coherence, that it stops abruptly and inconclusively instead of coming to a satisfactory resolution and that it provides no "solutions" for the problems it depicts. Putting aside as beyond settlement, the question of whether an artist need "solve" problems that engage him, I would like simply to point out that in an earlier study of Steinbeck's fiction I try to demonstrate that *The Grapes of Wrath* is not a collection of disjointed episodes but a carefully worked out story that depicts the conversion of the Joads from a violent, self-centered family concerned only with preserving and perpetuating the clan, to a group of individuals who have learned from their own bitter experiences that man's survival depends upon the suppression of selfish instincts and the recognition of the dignity of every individual. As I have previously argued, the tableau at the end of the story in which Rosasharn Joad offers her breast to a dying stranger, "marks the end of the story Steinbeck had to tell about the Joads. Their education is completed. They have triumphed over familial prejudices. What happens to them now depends upon the ability of the rest of society to learn the same lesson they have already learned." [1]

As far as the central narrative about the education of the Joads is concerned, *The Grapes of Wrath* is not even truly what I have defined as a social novel. It stresses the achievement of individualism as much as the works of Thomas Wolfe and depicts the necessity of each individual's educating and reforming himself, rather than the causes of a national disaster. If the Joads had not been caught up in the events of a particular time and place that had profoundly affected Steinbeck and troubled his public, we might more easily recognize that their story belongs with Shakespeare's *The Tempest* and other masterpieces of the travail and triumph of the human spirit.

The Grapes of Wrath is, however, deeply rooted in depression-ridden America. It not only depicts some of the most harrowing events of the period, but it is also the outstanding artistic embodiment of a point of view that paradoxically both preserved the United States and held back its progress during the economic crisis. Steinbeck's novel is more closely related to Faulkner's *The Hamlet* than one might casually suppose. Both not only deal with conditions that blighted the nation, but also reflect similar viewpoints toward the causes and cure of that blight.

It is not really true that Steinbeck proposes no solutions for the problems that he depicts. Artist rather than social theorist, he implies rather than spells out his prescriptions; and some of the best-intentioned social reformers appear to lack the subtle gift for deciphering metaphors. The hints that he gives, however, show that his novel, far from representing an unusual or distinctive point of view, rests upon the same basic assumptions (the term *philosophy* seems inapplicable to any such unsystematic thinking) as a substantial body of work produced by some conservative intellectuals of the era.

Conservative may seem a strange word to apply to the author of *The Grapes of Wrath*, which many truculent defenders of the shabby *status quo* denounced as radical when it was published. Yet even though the novel was enthusiastically received in Russia as evidence of American decadence, relations between Steinbeck and the pro-Communist intellectuals of the thirties had been strained since the publication in 1936 of *In Dubious Battle*, at the end of which Steinbeck had metaphorically accused Red agitators of what he—like Hawthorne—considered the unpardonable sin—the exploitation and destruction of human beings for the advancement of an abstract cause. Before his disappearance, Doc Burton, the most sympathetic character in the novel, explains to the principal representative of the Party: "There've been communes before, and there will be again. But you people have an idea that if you can *establish* the thing, the job'll be done.

Nothing stops, Mac. If you were able to put an idea into effect tomorrow, it would start changing right away. Establish a commune, and the same gradual flux will continue." Asked if he doesn't think "the cause" is good, he replies, "I want to see the whole picture—as nearly as I can. I don't want to put on the blinders of 'good' and 'bad,' and limit my vision." [2]

Throughout his work, Steinbeck has always maintained that consideration for the individual human being must be placed above any cause or party. From *The Pastures of Heaven* to *Cannery Row*, he stresses constantly the essential loneliness of the individual and the necessity of the individual's accepting the often unpleasant responsibility for his actions and decisions. Even if he is destroyed, like Danny in *Tortilla Flat*, it is better that he die a free agent than live the captive of any system. Conservative ideas about the individual and his relationship to government have been quite conspicuous in Steinbeck's recent works like *Sweet Thursday* and *The Short Reign of Pippin IV*, but this conservatism marks no abrupt shift in his thinking. Steinbeck, who has always been preoccupied with the relationship between the individual and the group, indicated in such early stories as "The Raid" and "The Vigilante" that he disapproved of what happened if the individual submerged himself in the group.

Those who found symptoms of Leftist thinking in *The Grapes of Wrath* must have accepted one of Steinbeck's character's sarcastic description of a Communist as "any son-of-a-bitch that wants thirty cents an hour when we're payin' twenty-five" (p. 407).[3] There are only two passages—both in interchapters—that could be mistaken for radical propaganda.

> If you who own the things people must have could understand this, you might preserve yourself. If you could separate causes from results, if you could know that Paine, Marx, Jefferson, Lenin, were results, not causes, you might

survive. But that you cannot know. For the quality of owning freezes you forever into "I," and cuts you off forever from the "we." (p. 206)

And the great owners, who must lose their land in an upheaval, the great owners with access to history, with eyes to read history and to know the great fact: when property accumulates in too few hands it is taken away. And that companion fact: when a majority of the people are hungry and cold they will take by force what they need. (p. 324)

Read carefully in context, however, neither passage advocates revolt nor gives the author's view of what *should* happen. In both he speaks as an observer, warning what *may* happen—what it *regrettably* appears *will* happen. These passages, like the novel as a whole, are not rabble-rousing speeches inciting an outraged proletariat to rise against its oppressors; rather they are warnings to a comfortable and negligent propertied class to awaken it to what is happening around it. *The Grapes of Wrath* in its treatment of contemporary events is a cautionary tale.

Steinbeck does in the fifth chapter of the novel denounce the impersonal and irresponsible course that American business has taken through the twenties and thirties, and he depicts sympathetically those who rail at the "ridiculousness of the industrial life" (p. 385). But critics have not been sufficiently cautious in avoiding the fallacy of the undistributed middle when categorizing Steinbeck. Far from joining ranks with the "proletarian" authors of the thirties who rallied enthusiastically to the Communist cause, Steinbeck served as a spokesman of a "third force."

This group held, in the words of Herbert Agar, whose collaborators on *Who Owns America?* (1936) have exhibited little appreciation of Steinbeck, that the American dream of the independence of the individual was being "derided" by two groups—"the communists, who say that any attempt to realize it must be vain, since the attempt would contradict the laws of Marx; second, by the friends of Big Business, who dishonor the dream by saying that it has been realized, that it lies all about us today." [4] The contributors to *Who Owns America?* sought an alternative to both communism and Big Business that would free the capitalist system from the stranglehold of monopoly. Their search, like Steinbeck's, led to the idealization of the independent yeoman.

This important aspect of Steinbeck's thought has been recognized by only two previous critics of *The Grapes of Wrath*. Joseph Fontenrose observes that Steinbeck's "'agrarian socialism' is really Chestertonian Distributivism, a society of small-scale farmers working their own plots," [5] and Chester Eisinger in the best analysis of the ideological underpinnings of the novel, "Jeffersonian Agrarianism in *The Grapes of Wrath*" argues that while a discussion of Jefferson's views "does not pretend to serve as an interpretation of the entire novel," it is closely associated "with what was apparently one of the primary motives for writing the book, the desire to protest against the harsh inequities of the financial-industrial system that had brought chaos to America in the thirties." [6]

Against Fontenrose's undeveloped assertion, it can be argued that while the parallel is basically sound, it is grossly oversimplified since Steinbeck and Chesterton operated from vastly different premises. Eisinger's cogent argument demands close scrutiny, but it does not suggest the extent of the effort in the thirties to win converts to an "alternative" to monopoly capitalism or communism that is too much limited when it is labeled simply "Jeffersonian."

Eisinger points out that the belief basic to Jefferson's doctrine is that "landed property held in freehold must be available to everyone" and that the independent farmer "acted in accordance with his own instincts or desires and rose or fell by virtue of his own efforts." It shared the primitivistic doctrine that "close contact with nature and with God makes and keeps men pure," whereas "the city is a cesspool of evil." [7] Steinbeck, Eisinger maintains, accepts and projects through his novel the notion that "the farmer draws spiritual strength as well as sustenance from the soil." [8]

In the fifth chapter that holds the key to the book's ideology, Steinbeck does have one of his anonymous migrants express what can only be described as the concept of a mystical union between a man and his soil.

> "Funny thing how it is. If a man owns a little property, that property is him, it's part of him, and it's like him. If he owns property only so he can walk on it and handle it and be sad when it isn't doing well, and feel fine when the rain falls on it, that property is him, and some way he's bigger because he owns it. Even if he isn't successful he's big with his property. That is so." (p. 50)

The real evil of corporate farming, Steinbeck clearly suggests, in a description of the driver of a tractor that is plowing up the tenants' farms for the remote and untouchable city corporation, is that it destroys this mystical bond between man and land.

> The man sitting in the iron seat did not look like a man; gloved, goggled, rubber dust mask over nose and mouth, he was a part of the monster, a robot in the seat.
>
> .   .   .   .
>
> He loved the land no more than the bank loved the land. . . . The driver sat in his iron seat and he was proud of the straight lines he did not will, proud of the tractor he did not own or love, proud of the power he could not control. And when that crop grew, and was harvested, no man had crumbled a hot clod in his fingers and let the earth sift past his fingertips. . . . The land bore under iron, and under iron gradually died; for it was not loved or hated, it had no prayers or curses. (pp. 48–49)

The blight of the corporate society as Steinbeck sees it is the same that Warren Beck points out Flem Snopes brought upon the Mississippi of Faulkner's *The Hamlet*—automatism. The city and the machine have broken the bond between man and the soil and have reduced man to a robot. Hence Steinbeck does not have his dispossessed farmers seek refuge in the city to which many had turned during agricultural depressions; rather they abandon their exhausted Midwestern soil in the hopes of claiming a new homestead in California where Ma Joad dreams that they "can get one of them little white houses" and "the little fellas go out an' pick oranges right off the tree" (p. 124). Both Faulkner's and Steinbeck's novels associate with the move from farm to city, the tragic havoc wrought by those who seek financial success rather than love.

Chester Eisinger notes in passing that the period of *The Grapes of Wrath* "saw also the growth of the back-to-the-farm movement and the proliferation of books guaranteeing independence, and even security, on five acres," [9] but writing at a time when many of the proponents of this back-to-the-soil movement were still vocal, he did not consider it necessary to linger over their tracts. *The Grapes of Wrath* has, however, because it is more than a single-minded tract, outlived the movement that it in part reflected. Today's readers are likely to regard Steinbeck as an isolated voice, and only by recalling some of the now largely forgotten expressions of similar sentiments can we understand his novel as a reflection of important patterns of social and economic thinking in the thirties.

ii

The basic notion of the virtue of rural life long antedated Jefferson's eighteenth century. Paul H. Johnstone, tracing the history of "the praise of husbandry," finds its literary origins (its actual origins must be lost in antiquity) in the writings of Hesiod, Xenophon, and Cato, the last of whom in what is considered the oldest extant prose work in Latin, declared farmers better citizens than city dwellers.[10] This philosophy enjoyed a great vogue among the writers of Rome's Augustan Age; and, although it lost its appeal during the Middle Ages, when most men were grubbing out dreary existences on farms, it was revived by those Renaissance writers who showed an enthusiasm for all things Classic. After flourishing in the sixteenth century, the notion of rural virtue declined in the seventeenth, but revived vigorously in the eighteenth, reaching its climax during the reign of George I. The principal propagators of the doctrine in England were Richard Bradley, Stephen Switzer, and John Lawrence, who in *Paradice Regain'd* (1728) "illustrated the moral that gardening was the key to the recovery of terrestrial happiness." Although as the century progressed, Johnstone continues, "State favor was concentrated upon urban industry and commerce rather than upon agriculture, and . . . country life and residence was generally considered a misfortune to be avoided whenever possible," rearoused enthusiasm was reflected in works like Goldsmith's "The Deserted Village" and Thomson's "The Seasons" and principally in the writings of Arthur Young.[11]

Meanwhile in France a group called the Physiocrats were trying to organize one of the pioneering efforts at economic theory around the passion for rural life. Although an English banker, Cantillon, and a French court doctor, Quesnay, are often given credit, respectively, for formulating and systematizing the physiocratic concepts, the man principally responsible for their enthusiastic reception in the late eighteenth century was Victor de Riqueti, Marquis de Mirabeau, stern parent of the outstanding orator of the French revolutionary movement. Presenting quite a different face to his reading public than he showed his family, Mirabeau began publishing in 1758 a commentary on Cantillon, *L'ami des hommes,* which advanced the notion that "the small cultivator was to be encouraged and held in honour; the idle consumer viewed with reprobation," ideas which Eisinger points out are specifically illustrated by Steinbeck in his depiction of poor and rich travelers. Mirabeau also held that "an unequal distribution of wealth is prejudicial to production, for the very rich are 'like pikes in a pond' who devour their smaller neighbours." [12] Mirabeau argued that the great landowners should live on their estates and stimulate their development and that a ministry of agriculture should be created to bring to farming "the succour of applied science." That Mirabeau, through his impassioned writing, was the principal propagator of physiocratic doctrines, is evidenced by the honors that he received from dignitaries like the King of Sweden and from his becoming known himself as "the friend of man." Yet, although physiocratic theories were carried into practice in three villages in Baden, Adam Smith was not unduly cynical when he said that the notions had never been tried out. Nor was there much emulation of the example offered in *The Rural Socrates*, by Hans Caspar Hirzel, of Kliyogg Gouyer of Wermetschweil, Switzerland, who exemplified everything that Xenophon had said Socrates commended in men distinguished for "prudence and understanding." The French translation of Hirzel's book was, however, enthusiastically recommended by Mirabeau, and the English translation was sponsored by Arthur Young.

Even though Jefferson became a friend of Pierre Samuel du Pont de Nemours, one of the principal disciples of the physiocrats and, ironically, father of the founder of one of America's largest corporations, Gilbert Chinard, who edited the men's correspondence does not think that Jefferson was influenced by the French doctrines, but rather hit upon them independently.

Jefferson's most explicit statement about rural virtue is the earliest of his preserved references to the subject. In his *Notes on Virginia*, he wrote:

> Those who labor in the earth are the chosen people of God, if ever he had a chosen people, whose breasts he has made his peculiar deposit for substantial and genuine

virtue. . . . While we have land to labour then, let us never wish to see our citizens occupied at a work-bench, or twirling a distaff. . . . The mobs of great cities add just so much to the support of pure government, as sores do to the strength of the human body.[13]

Several years later he wrote in the same strain to John Jay from Paris.

Cultivators of the earth are the most valuable citizens. They are the most vigorous, the most independent, and the most virtuous. . . . As long therefore as they can find employment in this line, I would not convert them into mariners, artisans, or anything else. . . . I consider the class of artificers as panders of vice and the instruments by which the liberties in a country are generally over-turned.[14]

Two years later, in 1787, in a letter to John Blair, he called "the pursuits of Agriculture, the surest road to affluence and best preservative of morals," and the next day he wrote to Washington, "The wealth acquired by speculation and plunder is fugacious in it's nature and fills society with the spirit of gambling. The moderate and sure income of husbandry begets improvement, quiet life, and orderly conduct both public and private." [15]

On such statements, what Eisinger calls the Jeffersonian myth has been erected, but Jefferson himself did not cling unalterably to these sentiments. Home from what must have seemed a depraved Paris and close to the soil once more, he showed that he had doubts even before the close of the eighteenth century about ideas that his followers still advocated in the twentieth. To Horatio Gates on February 21, 1798, Jefferson wrote, "How far it may lessen our happiness to be rendered merely agricultural, how far that state is more friendly to the principles of virtue & liberty, are questions yet to be solved." [16] By 1817 he was even less enthusiastic. To William Sampson he wrote:

I was once a doubter whether the labor of the Cultivator, aided by the creative powers of the earth itself, would not produce more value than that of the manufacturer, alone and unassisted by the dead subject on which he acted? . . . But the inventions of latter times, by labor-saving machines, do as much now for the manufacturer, as the earth for the cultivator. Experience too has proved that mine was but half the question. The other half is whether Dollars & cents are to be weighed in the scale against real independence? [17]

By the end of his life, however, Jefferson recognized that even the "real independence" of the agrarian life might be illusory. In a pathetic last letter to Madison written February 17, 1826, only a few months before his death, Jefferson, fearing that he might lose his beloved Monticello, observed:

the long succession of years of stunted crops, of reduced prices, the general prostration of the farming business, under levies for the support of manufactures & c., with the calamitous fluctuations of value in our paper medium, have kept agriculture in a state of abject depression which has peopled the Western States by silently breaking up those in the Atlantic and glutted the land market, while it drew off its bidders. In such a state of things, property has lost its character of being a resource for debts.[18]

Although he placed the blame for the calamitous agricultural situation upon the growth of industry, Jefferson recognized that however virtuous the life close to the soil might be, it was not in itself capable of preserving the individual's independence and integrity.

Jefferson's defection did not, however, deal the death blow to the ideas that he had earlier espoused. A similar view of the virtues of the agrarian life was advanced late in the nineteenth century by Pope Leo XIII, whose encyclicals have been called "the most important single contribution to catholic doctrine since the Middle Ages." [19] This first modern pontiff of the Roman Catholic church not to be burdened with the temporal administration of the Papal States, which Italy had absorbed in 1870, laid down the tenets of a new agrarianism in one of his most influential social encyclicals, *Rerum Novarum* (*Of New Things*), a statement about the condition of the working classes that vigorously attacks the increasingly influential doctrines of socialism.

Pope Leo thought that the appeals of this pernicious new movement might be countered by greater "distributive justice." He especially remarked that "the law . . . should favor ownership, and its policy should be to induce as many as possible of the humble class to become owners," since "if working people can be encouraged to look forward to obtaining a share in the land, the consequence will be that the gulf between vast wealth and sheer poverty will be bridged over and the respective classes brought nearer one another." He also argued that the policy would slow down migration, because "no one would exchange his country for a foreign land if his own afforded him the means of living a decent and happy life." [20]

There is no more reason to argue that Steinbeck was influenced by the *Rerum Novarum* than by physiocratic pronouncements, but it is interesting to note that when in the last of his newspaper accounts of conditions in the migrant camps, Steinbeck makes his only specific suggestions of immediate remedies for the situation, they parallel statements in the encyclical. Steinbeck's suggestions boil down to two: that labor unions regulate the use of migratory labor in agriculture and that the practice of encouraging an oversupply of labor in order to reduce wages be stopped.[21] Pope Leo had specifically observed that "the organization of workingman's associations be permitted and encouraged for helping each individual member to better his condition to the utmost in body, mind and property" and that "the rich must religiously refrain from cutting down workmen's earnings, whether by force, by fraud, or usurious dealings." [22]

If Pope Leo did not directly influence Steinbeck, he certainly did directly influence the "distributist" schemes of the "Chesterbelloc" as the neo-orthodox Britons G. K. Chesterton and Hilaire Belloc came to be collectively known. Under Belloc's influence, Chesterton became one of the principal propagandists for a "back-to-the-soil" movement in the twenties. The statement of Chesterton's distributist views in *The Outline of Sanity* (1927) proves to be little more than a verbiose and foggy statement of the ideas about the encouragement of small property holding expressed in the *Rerum Novarum*.

The practical program of the Distributists is hard to specify, for, as Maisie Ward, Chesterton's biographer, admits, "A most difficult question to answer is the degree of the League's success. Its stated aim was propaganda, the spreading of ideas." [23] Clearly the group favored "back to the soil" concepts calling for the creation of a large peasantry that would own its farms. In *The Outline of Sanity*, Chesterton argued:

> The primary case for the peasant is of a stark and almost savage simplicity. A man in England might live on the land, if he did not have rent to pay to the landlord and wages to pay to the labourer. He would therefore be better off, even on a small scale, if he were his own landlord and his own labourer.[24]

He proposed no specific laws or programs for making the peasant his own landlord and laborer, however. The most definite proposal in the book merely calls for a poll.

> We want to find out how many peasants there are, actual or potential, who would take over the responsibility of small farms, for the sake of self-sufficiency, of real property, and of saving England in a desperate hour. We want to know how many landlords there are who would now give or sell cheaply their land to be cut up into a number of such farms.[25]

The execution of some land redistribution program would

he felt be beneficial because "It is that satisfaction of the creative instinct in the individual that makes the peasantry as a whole content and therefore conservative." [26]

Thus far, as Joseph Fontenrose suggests, Steinbeck's arguments in *The Grapes of Wrath* parallel Chesterton's vaguely formulated scheme; when we consider, however, the fundamental assumptions underlying their concepts of land redistribution, the unbridgeable gap between them becomes apparent. Steinbeck would surely be chilled by Chesterton's quaintly affected use of the condescending term "peasant," and he would surely reject Chesterton's concept, as expressed in a chapter on "The Religion of Small Property," of the aim not just of distributism, but of all human endeavor.

> The time has come in every department, but especially in our department, to make once again vivid and solid the aim of political progress or colonial adventure. Even if we picture the goal of the pilgrimage as a sort of peasant paradise, it will be far more practical than setting out on a pilgrimage which has no goal. But it is yet more practical to insist that we do *not* want to insist only on what are called the qualities of a pioneer; that we do not want to describe merely the virtues that achieve adventures. We want men to think, not merely of a place which they would be interested to find, but of a place where they would be contented to stay. Those who wish merely to arouse again the social hopes of the nineteenth century must offer not an endless hope, but the hope of an end. Those who wish to continue the building of the old colonial idea must leave off telling us that the Church of Empire is founded entirely on the rolling stone. For it is a sin against the reason to tell men that to travel hopefully is better than to arrive; and when once they believe it, they travel hopefully no longer.[27]

As his other traditionalist leanings also suggest, Chesterton yearned for a static order and looked, as did Pope Leo XIII, to an economy based upon small independent farmers as the source of political and social stability.

Against this notion of the desirability of a fixed order must be placed Steinbeck's clearest statement of his own dynamic faith in *The Grapes of Wrath*.

> For man, unlike any other thing organic or inorganic in the universe, grows beyond his work, walks up the stairs of his concepts, emerges ahead of his accomplishments. This you may say of man—when theories change and crash, when schools, philosophies, when narrow dark alleys of thought, national, religious, economic, grow and disintegrate, man reaches, stumbles forward, painfully, mistakenly sometimes. Having stepped forward, he may slip back, but only half a step, never the full step back. . . . If the step were not being taken, if the stumbling-forward ache were not alive, the bombs would not fall, the throats would not be cut. Fear the time when the bombs stop falling while the bombers live—for every bomb is proof that the spirit has not died. (pp. 204–5)

Steinbeck shares those "social hopes of the nineteenth century," expressed in Tennyson's and Browning's poems, that the reach must exceed the grasp, and the ideas of William Faulkner, who said in Japan:

> I don't hold to the idea of a return. That once the advancement stops then it dies. It's got to go forward and we have got to take along with us all the rubbish of our mistakes and our errors. We must cure them; we mustn't go back to a condition, an idyllic condition, in which the dream [made us think] we were happy, we were free of trouble and sin.[28]

The difference between the views represented, on the one hand, by Chesterton and, on the other, by Steinbeck and Faulkner are probably most admirably summed up in a passage from one of Jefferson's letters to Du Pont de Nemours that has been called one of the "great ideas" of Western man: "We both consider the people as our children, and love them with parental affection. But you love them as infants whom you are afraid to trust without nurses; and I as adults whom I freely leave to self-